Nineteen Vagabond Nineteen Vag

Spring Manoeuvres

Peter Gilmour

Vagabond Voices
Glasgow

Published on 30 May 2015 by
Vagabond Voices Publishing Ltd.
Glasgow
Scotland

ISBN: 978-1-908251-43-5

Printed and bound in Poland

Cover design by Mark Mechan

Typeset by Park Productions

The publisher acknowledges subsidy towards
this publication from Creative Scotland

ALBA | CHRUTHACHAIL

For further information on Vagabond Voices, see the website:
www.vagabondvoices.co.uk

For Lil, Andrew and James

Spring Manoeuvres

I

Across the loch – smooth as glass this July morning –
a nasal American voice was barking out an order, over
and over again. "One, two, three, four – out!" For all the
response it got, the voice might have been out of con-
trol, playing some kind of game, trying out a new tannoy
system. Then it fell silent, the huge floating structure from
which it came falling silent too, dark and heavy in the mild
morning air, monumental, fantastic, a steel folly clamped
on tin. At its side nestled two submarines, injured whales
by a hospital ship, so black they weren't easy to see at first
but, once seen, drawing the eye remorselessly.

Douglas Low, standing by the lochside, drew his shoul-
ders back. The silence was more arresting than the nasal
voice had been, more arresting than an interrupted ren-
dering of The Star Spangled Banner before that (it was as
though it had been put on by mistake and abruptly taken
off again), more arresting even than the sight of a helicop-
ter taking off from a platform which had come out from
the side of the structure and then been retracted. It gave
Douglas time to take in the details. Square in shape, the
structure had turrets or watchtowers at each corner. One
side of the square was open, so that submarines could be
brought aboard for servicing. On the other sides, red and
yellow lights winked ceaselessly, as though to proclaim the
uniqueness of the structure and warn other craft to keep
their distance. Wires ran between two of the turrets, and
on top of the other two were radar discs, turning slowly. It
was, Douglas knew, complete, perfectly equipped for all it
had to do in peace and war, but he couldn't get over the

feeling that it was still in process of construction, that if he were to come back in several months' time he would find that it had grown, spread across the loch, gained cinemas and supermarkets, surgeries and chapels.

A loud hammering broke out. Soon noise and echo were heard almost simultaneously. Douglas turned to leave, picking his way through the beach detritus: tyres, rubber gloves, gas cylinders, cans, condoms, syringes, bottles, sanitary pads. The smell of the loch was not as he remembered it: there was something oily about it now, sickly. It looked different too, unclean, viscid. Why then were he and his wife, Edith, both sixty years old, thinking of retiring here? Why was he on his way to view a cottage?

The last eighteen months had been hard for them, and they were used to adversity. Edith's condition had worsened; she was now mostly in a wheelchair, often in pain. Douglas had developed angina, so that early retirement from teaching had been forced on him. A depression brought on by the angina had been deepened and prolonged by the loss of work and income. It had taken him half a year to come out of it, and then, for a few months, he was at the opposite extreme – edgy, impatient, manic almost. Behind his large oval spectacles his eyes glittered. Then he had calmed down. And now, since Edith had long been as determined to make the most of her time as she was uncertain how much remained, they had come a little closer, sharing a kind of highminded impatience.

They were agreed that at last they should live where they wanted to. The first stage in redeeming the years that remained. The city had been convenient so long as Douglas had worked there, but now that he was retired and their son, Larry, had grown up and gone away, there was nothing to hold them. Much that seemed essential, in fact, beckoned from the countryside. Clear night skies for Douglas' telescope, purer air for Edith's chest, silence for her meditation. The place that had come to Douglas' mind was a holiday place. Childhood. Long summers. Edith liked it too. With her belief that the only paradise was a threatened one, she was bound to respond to it, with its signs of war, the inevitability of war.

So it was that Douglas, jacket over his arm, set off up a narrow street overhung with hawthorn and laburnum, pacing himself as the doctors had told him to. The cottage had "panoramic vistas". That meant it would probably take in the American presence on the Holy Loch, and it might, Douglas suspected, if the wind was in a certain quarter, be touched by odours unknown to his childhood. It was more a rediscovery of lung power than an experience of weakness. Not the wrong kind of tiredness anyway. He gained the crest of the hill and, in a little hollow, saw the white L shaped cottage. There were trees behind it, a semi-circle of limes and ashes, a garden in front. The view would be panoramic indeed. He would be happy with it, even if it was crisscrossed several times a day by low flying fighters (fighters flying ahead of sound, submarines moving without sound). There was a small terrace on which they could have meals in the good weather and onto which, when he was out, Edith could wheel herself. (The cottage, he had been assured by the estate agents, was ideal for invalids, all on one level, steps neither at the front nor the back, French windows at the back giving onto a lawn.) High and peaceful on its hill, yet not too isolated, connected to the road down which Douglas was walking by a short drive.

It had been empty for some months, the owner having died. A young woman from the estate agency, wearing a bottle green uniform with the agency's name on it, greeted Douglas, ticked his name off on a list, and handed him a schedule. Then launched into a little talk about the property. At the slightest sound of jets, however – but without ceasing to talk – she made as if to duck, crouch, cover her ears.

"The jets bother you?" Douglas asked.

"A bit. When they come over, I feel I'll be flattened. No doubt I'll get used to it."

The cottage still had its furniture, heavy antique furniture mainly, thick carpets, large, brightly coloured vases, tall bookcases full of books, standard lamps. Douglas liked it so much, could so easily see himself and Edith there, that he became talkative. Since his illness, he had been asking questions, compulsively at first, more moderately now (as if, through questions, he believed he could rehabilitate himself). He questioned the young woman. Did she get nervous, waiting around in remote cottages? How many cranks and eccentrics did she have to put up with? Did she resent having to wear a uniform? Stalled by so many affable enquiries, the young woman stopped in the large kitchen – alive at this moment with light and the shadows of trees – and reached into her pocket for a silver name badge. Pinned to her lapel, it said her name was Jennifer, and seemed to authorise her to speak.

"Most of the questions I'm asked are about the house. Don't you like it?"

"On the contrary. I like it very much. I must arrange to bring my wife down. She's disabled, you see; I didn't want to bring her all this way if it wasn't suitable."

"There was a disabled gentleman along to see it the other day. He was quite young."

Douglas looked into the back garden, squinting as from the effort to see the house through Edith's eyes. He wondered if it would be here that she died. Probably. Then himself. He prayed not the other way round.

The last of five houses they'd lived in as a married couple.

"You've a good chance," Jennifer said.

"I beg your pardon?"

"Of securing the property. There's not been much interest. The area, you see …"

"The Americans …"

"Yes. In the event of … well, you'd be the first to go."

Douglas laughed.

"A minute or two before Glasgow."

"I take your point," Jennifer said, fiddling with her name badge. "Still, people are uneasy. If you like it though …"

"I do."

"Then it's a bargain; the same cottage elsewhere would be much more."

"No doubt."

His heart (not one of the sensations to worry about though) turned and fluttered with the thought that while immense skills were employed in keeping war at bay, no amount of skill could raise Edith from her wheelchair or heal his heart.

"What would you do with your last few minutes, Jennifer?" he asked. "Oh, make it half an hour."

"I'd like to be with my boyfriend."

"Holding hands or all the way?" It was out before Douglas could stop it.

She smiled, but made it clear she wouldn't be drawn any further. Any further himself, Douglas knew, and he would be up against the dilemma which in one form or another had been stalking him for years: of the two women in his life, which would he like to spend his last moments with? Would he find, when the time came, that it was an unreal question, an adolescent dilemma? Or would it really count?

"Let's see the back garden then," he said.

He stood aside while Jennifer tried to open the French windows. They were stuck. She kicked off her high heels and gave her full weight to the task. Still they wouldn't budge. Crouching, she tried again, buttocks straining. It wasn't so much the windows, Douglas thought, as their conversation: he had unnerved the poor girl with talk of annihilation, final moments.

"It doesn't matter," he said, "we can walk round."

Suddenly the French windows opened, Jennifer finding herself outside, on a patio, in stocking soles, Douglas, following, unable to resist the temptation to stop, pick up the shoes and hand them back gallantly.

Out of breath, irritated, Jennifer wobbled as she put them on.

"Don't worry," Douglas said, a hand out to steady her. "Nothing sticks forever."

"Are you a gardener?" It was obviously what she asked at this stage.

"I was, quite a keen one too. Recently though I've had heart trouble; I've been taking it easy. Perhaps too easy. Maybe with a new garden around me I'll be inspired."

He stood with his hands on his hips, sports jacket pushed back, breathing evenly. He didn't think Jennifer believed he had heart trouble and there were times when he found it difficult to believe himself. Just now, climbing the hill, excited by smells of bark and sap and blossoms, he had been tempted to try himself out. A little canter. He had been warned not to overreach himself, of course, to be aware of limits at all times. But the thought of limits agreed upon by the doctors exasperated him: he felt driven to test them. Which gave him energy. Strategies for playing safe, however, did not.

His manner in the garden therefore was one which had recently become characteristic, shoulders back, one foot in front of the other, careful breathing, an air of slightly strained attention.

"You look fine to me," Jennifer said.

"I am, I'm sure." He looked up and away.

There was a clothes line in the back garden, strung between three rusty poles. The grass was long and thick, the ground even. They went round the side of the cottage by a gravel path to the front garden. Here the lawn was even too and the path which bisected it, running from the front door to the garden gate, broad and flat. Beyond the garden gate though there were three steps. He would have to make one of his ramps. Vaguely miming someone pushing a wheelchair, he walked from the front door to the garden gate and back again, Jennifer standing with arms folded, watching. At the front door he turned to look at the view. Give or take a foot or two, it would be Edith's view. There was no sign of the floating structure, not even of its turrets and radar discs. (No doubt, were he to strike out beyond the garden, they would quickly come into sight.) What he saw in the distance was the far shore of the loch, wooded hills behind, firs and Caledonian pines.

"Ever pushed a wheelchair, Jennifer?"

"Never."

"If you do it often, it gets so you can't go anywhere without checking it for wheelchairs."

"I can imagine it."

"Spies for the disabled."

Douglas couldn't see it yet but he could hear it: a helicopter approaching from the north. A regular thudding within the overall din of the engine, echoes following the contours of the hills. In the lee of the hill behind the cottage it seemed to hover then, manoeuvring. Crouched, Douglas felt a kind of primitive longing: to be deafened by the helicopter, trapped, darkened by its shadow. Suddenly then, as though shot from the hill, catapulted, it was above them, turning this way and that, the tops of the garden trees blowing, shaking. For a second Douglas lost the sun as he tried to make out the markings. All he was aware of was a dark shape, shape and shadow inseparable, the racket making him feel they should fall to their knees.

Jennifer had seen heads, faces, and was smiling, as if this somehow made it bearable.

"I saw them. They were reading a map or something."

"Lost their way, d'you suppose?" Still crouched, Douglas realised he was bathed in sweat. "Do they come over often?"

"In three days, Mr Low, this has been the only one."

"You give me your word? No estate agent's bullshit?"

"I do. It's mainly very peaceful. Really it is."

Douglas turned aside to deal with his shirt, stuck to his back and caught up around his waist. The helicopter was over the loch now, hovering.

He hadn't imagined it would be so hard to find the house in which, for five successive years in the late forties, early fifties, he had spent his summer holidays. It was hard enough to find the street. Only the smells were familiar: dry grass and cut grass, a brininess in the air, sap. Was this the garden in which he had played with his brother, or that? Were these the trees they had climbed? Was it here, behind this bush, that they had crouched in the long evenings, spying on lovers in the lane? The name at least would tell him. When he came upon it though it was carved on wood and suspended from the branch of a tree. Forty years ago it had been on the gate, he was sure, but the gate was gone, the gate posts too. The effect was to give the house the air of a false claimant, some crude modern imitation of the original. OAKVILLA: the name didn't seem to refer much beyond the white wood on which it had been carved.

It was as if he had experienced the house and garden in terms of sounds and movements, and now there was silence, stillness. Or remembered them in certain lights and from certain angles and now the light was different, the angle too. He took a few steps up the drive, not really believing he was going to drop suddenly into glad familiarity. He didn't. Almost now he didn't want it anyway. Almost now dreaded it.

He went on. To his right, in the middle of a sloping lawn, was a monkey puzzle tree, beyond it, framed by two cherry trees, a greenhouse. Its windows were cracked and dirty and cobwebbed and it seemed both too small for anyone to work in and too small for the garden. He thought he remembered the terrace which led up to the house, but he had seen so many like it, it didn't arrest him. The porch also he felt was familiar but what mainly struck him were the grey lace curtains. So he proceeded, stopping and starting, in and out of a sense that he had been here before, until he stood by the front door. It was ajar, and there was a vague smell of cooking, a sound within as of pages or papers being flipped over by a breeze, agitated.

His impulse was to enter and wander about. As if the house was open to all. He listened for some moments, but hearing nothing human, moved round the side of the house, past windows. Through the first he saw a bedroom, plain and white and with an arrangement of dolls and teddy bears on a high bed; through the second, a boxroom, gloomy and cluttered; through the third – an open window – a living room with an old man asleep in an armchair. He was slumped to one side, snoring, clasped hands rising and falling on his stomach, mouth open. Moving on, Douglas came to the back of the house and another open door, through which, immediately and very clearly, he saw down and across a corridor and into the room in which the old man was sleeping. The back of his head was visible, the ears especially, but the snoring had either stopped or couldn't be heard from here. From here though, Douglas felt, his sleep appeared peaceful, with none of the suggestions of tension he had noticed through the open window. He thought he heard him start to snore again, but it was only a bluebottle, trapped between window panes. Then that ceased, silence returning as if it would never again be broken and as if the stately ticking of a grandfather clock somewhere in the depths of the house was simply there to enhance it.

More windows round the other side of the house.

Impossible to tell whether the rooms were just tidy or unoccupied. In one there was a long line of shoes in a window recess, in another a cot as well as a bed. Back on the terrace, he glimpsed the top of the submarine base – turrets, radar discs, high tech rigging, a flag he couldn't remember having seen earlier. It hung limp and dead in the windless noon, for some reason making Douglas feel that if he were to live here he might grow used to the base.

Then he spotted an old woman standing at the bottom of the drive, carrier bags about her, some toppled over, contents spilled. She was panting, one hand to her side, digging into it, the other repeatedly lifting a strand of hair from her face and placing it behind her ear. It would be the shock of seeing him on the terrace, Douglas supposed, that had confounded her, stopped her in her tracks. He walked jovially towards her, smoothing back his hair, aware that she was soaked in sweat, her dress sticking to her, rucked up a little. Distressed amongst her purchases. When her laboured breathing allowed her to, though, she smiled, quite a welcoming smile too.

"I spent some childhood holidays here," Douglas said.

"Lots did, it seems."

"It's not as I remember it though."

"If you were to meet yourself as you were then," the old lady mused, "you'd not recognise yourself either." Her breathing was returning to normal, allowing her to look at Douglas pleasantly and directly.

"Do you live here now?"

"We've been here some twenty-five years, my husband and I. My goodness it's hot." She made as if to retrieve her groceries.

"Here, let me help."

The old lady pulled her dress up to give herself freedom to bend. Careless of how she looked, then, she placed her feet wide apart and, like one doing exercises, stooped left and right, picking up her groceries and tossing them one by one into the bags. Douglas got down on one knee, reaching for oranges and apples and potatoes and avocados, thinking that probably each day something ridiculous and unfortunate like this happened to the old lady.

"My goodness it's hot," she said again, as if it explained more than the younger generation would ever understand. "My goodness."

Carrying two bags in one hand, three in the other, Douglas walked with her up to the house.

"I saw an old gentleman asleep in a back room," he said.

"My husband, Charles. I keep him asleep as long as I can because when he wakes he just complains."

"What about?"

"The Americans, the jeeps, the heat, the cost of living, the fact that the children hardly write any more, the sight of my varicose veins."

"Does he complain about noise, the noise of the aircraft?"

"Actually no. For all there's a base here, it's not that noisy. It's quite silent, in fact. Maybe that's one of the problems."

"A silent base." Douglas stood with the old lady by the front door, hoping she would invite him in. "I hope you don't think I was snooping ..."

"Not at all. I'd ask you in only it would be sure to wake Charles and I do want to avoid that."

"I quite understand," Douglas replied, turning with a wave to walk down to where, on the foreshore, about a mile away, under a tree, he had parked his car.

II

They moved into the cottage in late September. It was lovely autumn weather. Even more deeply than they had anticipated, however, the move exhausted them. For weeks they rose in mid-morning and were back in bed by eight or nine. Their days were formless, the cottage appearing able to resist all their attempts to order it, make it their own. They went for drives, but in spite of the beautiful weather came back discouraged, to half unpacked crates and boxes, to piles of books and clothes, crockery and carpets, pictures.

Partly because of the disorder, Edith had difficulty getting about. But only partly. Some of the corners were tighter than she had known, and one of the corridors – Douglas hadn't noticed it before – was on a little slope, so that, depending on whether it was going up or down, the wheelchair went too slowly or too fast. Quite often Edith called out for help, her voice high and exasperated. Douglas had to steel himself to respond, so dejected was he, so troubled by a sense that in moving here they'd made a bad mistake. Once he went so far as to ignore her, something he'd never done before.

Going to her at last, however, he had found her in tears, fallen so far forwards in the wheelchair it was as if she was trying to get out. The wheelchair was trapped between two crates. Consoling her, rearranging her wasted legs under the tartan rug, he had found energy. Enough, at least, to have an idea. They wouldn't think of the cottage as their last home.

They wouldn't think of anywhere like that. They would

give it a year, and then, if they were still miserable, they would move back to the city. Weren't all but a few decisions provisional, reversible?

It helped; they ceased to feel so trapped. Settling Edith in the car before one of their drives, he thought she looked lighter, expectant. He felt lighter himself. She was looking after her hair again, twisting it into a bun and fixing it on top of her head. During their first days in the cottage she had borne herself as if the endurance of pain might be all there was. She had let her hair go, all over her shoulders, a mass of greyness which gave the wheelchair the appearance of having wings, Douglas thought, a giant beetle which would never fly.

In time, he was confident, she would resume her meditation. Her transcendental outlet, as she called it. And in time he would find a place for his telescope, searching the night sky passionately again, as for reasons why they were here, in this cottage above the Holy Loch. Because of the pain of her condition, Edith slept badly. If she hadn't woken by eleven, Douglas would wake her. It was unspoken now between them that he should do this. Only on special occasions was he allowed to wake her earlier.

One such occasion seemed to be a day in late October. Douglas had slept well, and of course it might have been just this: he had the energy for the day, so the day appeared significant. Independently of this, the day had splendour, he thought, a golden stillness over loch and hills, as if, overnight, the Almighty had purged the earth of all clamour and grossness.

Sitting on her bed, he placed the cup of tea on the bedside table. He took her hand in his and said it was time to get up. Waking her could take time, what with her broken nights and all the sleeping pills and painkillers she took. Mainly he did it by talking to her, by taking her hand and squeezing it, on bad mornings by shaking her gently, raising his voice a little.

This was a bad morning. She had to be shaken several times and even then didn't quite waken. Often he was tempted to let her sleep, for waking meant waking to pain. That tightening of the lips (loose in sleep, as though slackened by the drugs), tensing of the jaw. Such a troubled stirring. He would try to fill the waking moments with kind and pleasant remarks, whispered and murmured promises, assurances. It was not just pain she was waking to. Certainly not. The birds were in strange chorus, the light remarkable, he had never seen such light, it reminded him of Turner, would he put on some music, Vaughan Williams, Mozart, Bach? He had to be inventive, this morning unusually so. He might have had a definite surprise for her, so determinedly did he lead her over the threshold into pain and consciousness.

Once she was awake, he would lift her, a little at a time, from a lying to a sitting position, until she was propped against three pillows. If it was cold, he would offer her a cardigan. Today it wasn't. If it had been a bad awakening, he would help her lift her mug of tea – as today, slowly and falteringly – to her lips. Whatever he did, she was grateful, unspoken between them too the knowledge that without him she wouldn't be able to start her days at all.

"This is most welcome," she said, holding the mug, easing her shoulders into the pillows. "Most welcome."

Douglas smiled, wondering at these simple expressions of gratitude, their power to relax him, make him happy.

Not so when she theorised. The importance of meditation. The higher view of illness. Illness within the cycle of being. Stages, levels. Reincarnation. He dreaded such talk, thinking it a symptom of anxiety and distress. At her best she had no need of it, no need at all.

There was none this morning. Soon it was time for her pills. He would allow twenty minutes to pass before reaching for them (the blue pills, the white pills, the red). They were unpleasant on the tongue and he didn't want her tea ruined. Then – whether she could have done it her-self or not – he would lift a glass of water to her lips. It was an attention she particularly appreciated, he wasn't quite sure why, for it made her seem weaker than she was, or perverse, a difficult patient. Perhaps it was simply the pills – alarm at having to take so many.

"And how are you?" she asked, her voice, as always in the mornings, a little rough, hoarse. "No tightness?"

"No. I seem to be alright now."

Just after the move, he had sometimes felt unwell, a slight tightness in the chest, breathlessness, but the doctor had reassured him: it was only fatigue, tension.

There had been Edith's reassurances, too. She had the view that if you had honestly fathomed your world and seen how to live in it you would know ease, good health. Most illnesses were invited, she thought. He didn't think he really understood such views, but he never said so. And he had never asked her how they applied to herself. Why press her, aspiring as she did to a peace and purity untouched by the wretchedness of her body?

"You look as if you've something up your sleeve," Edith said.

"I have."

"You feel we've lost time to make up for here?"

"Exactly that. Those bad weeks back there."

"Tell me then."

"I thought of hiring a boat."

"A boat? What kind of a boat?"

"A rowing boat or small motor boat."

"I don't think you're quite ready for a rowing boat."

"A boat with an outboard motor then."

"Yes."

"We can take a look at the loch, pay our respects."

"There'll be restrictions, I suppose," Edith said, looking out of the window.

"I'm sure of it, but for some reason I think we should proceed as if there aren't."

"Yes." Edith nodded firmly. "I agree."

He lifted her from the bed into the wheelchair, pushing her to the bathroom, right up to the toilet seat with its support rails. There, as always, he asked her if she could manage now by herself, moving away as he did so. Always she said that she could manage. It seemed wrong not to ask though, wrong not to ask again ten minutes later. But he could surprise himself at these times: a little impersonal, accents of strained civilised enquiry, as if he'd address any disabled person so.

Once she had been able to propel the wheelchair quite vigorously. But the disease had spread. Now she did it awkwardly, arms trembling with the effort. Douglas hated to see it, but hated also the way she looked when he was being too solicitous. Between too much and too little he had to balance himself. He wouldn't allow her to go to and from the lavatory by herself, for example. But he would allow her to move from the toilet seat to the wheelchair to the door and then through it. And whenever he was out, of course, she would move about a bit, here and there, gasping, he imagined, bent forwards, eyes fixed on whatever spot she was determined to reach.

Back in the bedroom, there were two preparations: Douglas preparing to dress Edith, Edith preparing to be dressed. He had been doing it for about a year, but was still uneasy. His attempts to ritualise it so that it passed quite pleasantly had failed. They never seemed far from degradation, the two of them: on both sides the utmost patience and good humour was required. And, even then, there was embarrassment.

He had once rejoiced in her body, but did so no longer. Pity now or terror, quiet terror. She had once rejoiced in his hands, but did so no longer. On bad days she could hate them: the insult of their deftness.

This day it was different. Douglas was astonished. From a pile beside her, she selected the clothes one by one and handed them to him almost playfully. And in the same order, as if the game today was total obedience, he dressed her, now moving her onto one buttock, now onto the other, to put her pants on, now lifting one arm, now the other, to put her singlet on, then her blouse, now easing on her tights, now her slacks.

Nothing was said, but it was a silence without strain. The bright sun brought out the silver in her hair, the slack flesh at her neck and jaw, but did so kindly, as if in time it might bring aid.

He thought if only it could be like this every morning. If only he could always feel that he was dressing her for a pilgrimage. What had they done to deserve it?

He didn't doubt that there would be many more mornings when she cursed him, cursed God, longed for death, and when, to stop himself abandoning her half dressed, he bit his lip, whistled, stared out of the window.

The water on the other side of the loch was motionless, the wooded hills beyond – autumnal browns and reds, intense evergreens – clear as though magnified. There were hardly any sounds.

"The Americans must have moved out," Edith joked.

"It's like a Sabbath, only it's Thursday."

The wheelchair rumbled on the ramp Douglas had made for it outside the garden gate. The rumbling echoed slightly over to their left. He parked the wheelchair by the car and opened the passenger door. Getting her into and out of the car was one of the hardest tasks. If she was alive in four or five years' time it would probably be beyond him. She mightn't be, of course. Nor might he. Both dead and gone but the ramp still standing.

"Have you met any Americans yet?" Edith asked.

"No, but I've seen lots about – mainly getting into taxis actually."

"I can't imagine the base ever going."

"That's right. You can't put the clock back."

"It'll always be there, in some form or other."

"Like death and the sun," Douglas said, "and like death and the sun not really seen."

Edith laid a hand on his arm.

"Some may achieve the direct gaze, you know. We can't rule it out."

She took her hand away and smiled, as if just to make the point had encouraged her.

Douglas nodded. She to her version of faith, he to his. Leave it at that.

Edith fell silent. Douglas glanced at her, wondering if she was going to turn inwards, caught up by some incommunicable part of her inner life, say nothing for an hour or so, mouth twitching occasionally, eyes filling with pain. She wasn't. She laughed instead and said how autumn was her favourite time, how simplifying and clarifying she found it.

It was narrow and twisting, the way down to the coast road. They went through dappled sunlight and between high walls and hedges. After it, the coast road was strikingly open, almost shockingly so. Edith craned her neck to look at the base.

"It's so big," she said, "and so dark. So obscene! Too easy to say that though."

"What do we have but words where such things are concerned?" Douglas asked.

"Are words enough?"

"Well, there are marches, I suppose."

"Marches? I can't go on marches."

"I'll take you. We'll go together."

Once again he glanced at her, fearing withdrawal, once again was surprised. The prospect of the boat trip was obviously exciting her, keeping her from brooding. Wouldn't it be good if he could think up two or three excursions a week? Adventures. They could build up a store of them, selecting from it according to their moods and desires, the weather and the season. It would help him too, for wasn't it true that since thinking of the boat trip first thing this morning he'd paid little attention to what was going on in the region of his heart?

The boat hire place was a disused pier with a hut on it, on the door of the hut a notice: "Enquiries Within'. Douglas knocked lightly and stood back. Eventually a young man in dungarees and wellington boots appeared, half dancing to pop music.

"Just yourself?"

"My wife too. She's disabled."

"You can have Lucy-Ann. That one there." Without moving from the doorway, the young man pointed. "No trespassing, of course."

"Which means?"

"Keep clear of the base at all times. Stay outside the blue and red buoys."

"Alright."

Beside the pier was a concrete landing stage to which, while Douglas steered the wheelchair down from the car, the young man brought the boat. With difficulty, gasping a little, Douglas got Edith out of the wheelchair and into his arms (always in his arms she felt light, too light). The young man was in the boat now, standing, smiling, arms raised to receive Edith. Theatrically ready for his good deed. Between them the loch sucked and lapped, smelling of oil and seaweed. He gave Edith over. Easily, then, almost playfully, as if he might have chucked her in the air and caught her again, the young man had Edith settled in the stern. She was smiling.

The young man told Douglas how to operate the boat, assured him that if he got into difficulties he would be rescued, and then, yanking the motor into life, jumped ashore. A cloud of blue smoke drifted behind them as, nervous now, Douglas steered the boat past the end of the pier and out into the loch. To stay out for an hour or so, alert at all times to other craft, then bring the boat back safely to the pier and landing stage no longer seemed that simple. He wondered at the young man's readiness to trust him. Edith was unconcerned, however, smiling, looking about her. He smiled back, but what he was thinking was that in this attempt to give shape and purpose to their retirement he had overreached himself.

Then he began to relax. The boat was easy to steer and he found he could control its speed as well as he could that of his car. Aiming at the horizon, the open sea, an area of glare and whiteness, he accelerated until the bow lifted. Through the roar of the engine he heard Edith laughing – a rare sound these days. Then she was pointing, pointing and laughing, first at their boiling wake, then at a cabin cruiser which was approaching, flags flying. He gave it a wide berth, looking to see who was in charge, seeing no-one, the flags the only signs of life, flags of many sizes and colours.

The power of the boat rose through the tiller. As though to share in it, Edith kept a hand on Douglas' arm. One moment her delight appeared almost savage, he thought; the next, wondering, reflective, grateful.

Why shouldn't he put her in charge for a while? Go and sit by himself in the bow? Through the roar of the engine he gestured his intention. She looked uncertain but allowed her hand to be drawn to the tiller. Both their hands were there then, sharing the juddering, the agitation. Then Douglas moved away. Immediately the boat went violently to the left, a kind of fierce dipping arc. Douglas was thrown sideways, Edith against him.

It took him a minute or two to regain control. He resumed their original course, towards the open sea. Both shores seemed very far away. The hills and woods, as though flattened by the weight of sky, were barely recognisable. Mere strips. They moved as through an overarching glare of whiteness, Douglas imagining a deep ocean brininess to the air and spray. Seagulls swooped, huge birds, their cries piercing the roar of the engine.

Soon Edith indicated that she wanted to try again. This time the boat moved only slightly to the left, Edith quickly correcting it. Douglas sat away from her, simulating a confidence he didn't quite feel, wondering at the contrast between the harsh roar of the boat and the delicacy of its handling.

Suddenly the engine spluttered, recovered, spluttered again, cut out. In an overwhelming silence they found themselves drifting seawards. Ahead they could see nothing, behind almost nothing either. The day had a brightness which seemed to defeat vision rather than aid it. For several moments, shading their eyes, neither spoke: it could almost have been their intention to drift like this, Douglas felt, so calmly were they sitting, Edith looking to starboard, he to port.

"He said something about overheating. We just wait."

"I don't mind," Edith said, and he saw that she meant it.

He gave the engine ten minutes, then yanked the cord. It burst into life.

After the drifting, however, motor power was a disappointment. Douglas missed the sounds, of birds and water, missed the silence. He went seawards for a time, then turned and headed home.

Presently they spotted the base at the head of the loch. Going out, they hadn't been aware of it. They slowed down, the engine making a put-putting sound now. A rubber tyre floated past, a life jacket, shards of timber. In a sudden patch of clear water they saw fish, in another, streaks of oil. Then there was the rainbow discoloration of petrol, a lot of this. Low sounds, as of barking or hammering, came to them. A whistle blew.

Suddenly Douglas switched off the engine and they were drifting again.

"At this rate," Edith said, "we'll collide with the base

and be arrested. If we plead engine failure, though, what can they do?"

"There are oars for emergencies."

"I'm not having you row."

"We just drift?"

"Why not?" Edith was smiling. "Why should anyone suspect a cripple and a man with a heart condition?"

They sat together at the stern, drifting down the loch to the base whose platforms and turrets and lights and antennae were becoming clearly visible. A soundless drifting, a move not so much off course as into another dimension. On the coast road Douglas saw a car, but for some reason didn't hear it, as if it too were drifting. Beside him, Edith didn't move, hadn't moved since he'd switched off the engine. She looked implacable, eyes set in the mournful stare he associated with meditation. A soul going through levels, seeking painlessness. The signs were she was meditating now: shoulders back, chin slightly raised, hands clasped, eyes hooded. Aware of some agitation in himself, Douglas tried to imitate her, but the restlessness remained. He wondered at her readiness to let chance decide where they went. He felt her willing him to accept it too, forcing him, will upon will.

The boat was drifting straight at the base. He would have preferred it to be going slightly to the left. But he did nothing.

"Just sit still." She spoke with the entranced slowness that came upon her when she was giving high advice. "Have faith. Our schemes are petty. Providence is all."

"If we damage the boat we'll have to pay for it."

"So?"

"I'd rather not have to."

"Douglas." A dreamy rebuke.

"Anyway, I don't think our allies are just going to sit there and let us crash into them."

"Wait and see." Her tone was sweet and sure.

They passed through a line of buoys, the boat still aimed at the base, what looked like the submarine bay. Edith's eyes were completely shut now; she looked almost peaceful. (Douglas could never see the point of this, of not looking. However hellish, the details.) A red light began to flash high up on one of the platforms and he wondered if it had anything to do with them, their nearness. For they were near now. He felt rather than saw the shadow of the base: it shut out the sun. The acoustic changed: sounds seemed either to issue from the submarine bay or be drawn into it. Then Douglas saw a submarine inside, black in the black belly, five or six men working on it. Now they were near enough to read signs and markings, to hear an insistent whirring sound, snatches of laughter, conversation.

Near enough to see pairs of binoculars trained on them, a man on the top deck standing with an upraised flag. When the flag was brought down – as it was, with a shout – a siren sounded and a small craft shot towards them, its occupants standing to attention, the most exaggerated attention Douglas thought he had ever seen.

"Open your eyes, Edith, for Christ's sake. They're coming!"

"Don't worry; they can't do much."

"Oh but they can! We're in American waters."

The craft, occupants still at attention, circled them so quickly and so many times it was as if that was its aim – to keep them trapped and helpless in the circle of its own speeding. Then it slowed, circling inwards, bobbing and lifting, stopping about a yard away. A high nasal voice, as of one arrested in late boyhood, asked them to explain themselves.

"We were out for a trip," Douglas said, "when the engine failed."

"What are those oars for?"

"Rowing is out of the question," Edith replied. "My husband has heart trouble and I'm disabled."

"What are your names?"

"What are they to you?" Edith asked.

"You're obliged, madam, to supply them." Saliva came from the young officer's mouth.

"Oh? Who says?" she asked.

"Clause twenty-seven, section b, the NATO Naval Agreement." He was about to quote from this when Douglas raised his hand. "Douglas and Edith Low, local residents." He spoke with a kind of dismissive quietness.

"Well, Mr and Mrs Low, I've got news for you. You'll be towed ashore immediately. A complaint will be filed and in all probability a charge made."

"Do what you like," Edith said.

He moved from attention and by doing so released the others from it too. A rope was attached to the bow of the hired boat and in a violent and peremptory way Douglas and Edith were towed away. All seemed calculated to insult and humiliate, Douglas thought: the scream of the engine, the high speed, the occupants of the craft at attention again. It was done so well he suspected it was done frequently.

The young man at the boat hire place came out to watch, arms folded.

"More prisoners," he said. "You must be proud of yourselves."

"We do our job."

"What about my dinghy then? If it's not back by next week, there'll be trouble."

The Americans ignored him. Bolt upright in their craft, they sped across the water to the base, disappearing round the back of it.

"Home to mother," the young man said, arms out to receive Edith. "You've no idea."

That evening, after sleeping for most of the afternoon, Edith said she wanted to meditate. She asked to be pushed into the bay window of the living room. (She often began by looking out of windows. Whatever the view, it could entrance, apparently.) The mood was on Douglas to lose himself too, but not in this way. Against a background of inner darkness, he imagined, Edith's insights would glow and flare, on very good days become foreground, all there was. But the only dark background he knew was that of the night sky. And that could be background or foreground according to whether you saw the stars as peeping through the darkness from below or piercing and dominating it from above, like jewels. Either way, to study it was to enter it and to enter it was to be changed, to be lightened somehow. The "I" which looked through telescopes at stars not as they were but as they had been thousands of years ago knew vertigo, certainly, but also awe. And for a time could be forgivingly at ease with its world.

Tonight it was too cloudy for stars. Still tense from the boat trip, he detached the telescope from its tripod and went outside, passing the window where Edith was meditating. He walked through the back garden, climbed a stile, started up the hill behind the cottage. A wind was getting up. At the top of the hill he turned and faced the loch. Horribly floodlit, the base was visible below him. He raised his telescope. Apparently the submarine was still being worked on. He had the odd fancy that attempts were being made to encourage it, persuade it to leave the base for the dark waters of the loch, the sea beyond.

Next he turned the telescope on the cottage, on Edith meditating. Anyone seeing her would have thought she was asleep, but Douglas was prepared to believe that in meditation you could reach certain depths, and that this was where Edith was. More charitable to think it, at least, than to suppose her asleep. More comforting too.

The wind roared in the trees behind him. An owl hooted – the first he'd heard since coming here.

III

For a day or two after an excursion Edith would have to rest, and Douglas would see to it that she did so. Such days could work to his advantage. Long practice had made it possible for him to combine nursing his wife with being free of her. If asked, in fact, he would probably have said that it was the second which made the first possible. And wouldn't have minded being thought hard. Not at all. Not now. You did what you could; you struck balances.

There were also the games. The more, watching from the wheelchair, she detected, or thought she detected, mere dutifulness in him, the more he felt challenged to make it seem otherwise. He had to keep a step ahead of her, as she, he supposed, strove to keep a step ahead of him. On bad days he feared that he only smiled when he thought he had deceived her, she when she thought she had caught him out.

Since retirement, the most difficult day – the one on which he was both most excited and most uneasy – had been the one before he met Helen. In the city, this had been once a week, sometimes twice, but since coming to the Holy Loch he hadn't met her at all. Now a meeting had been arranged. Six weeks had elapsed since the last one, their longest separation since they had met, eleven years ago. A passionate need and eagerness to see her had built up in him. To contain this, to keep control, he had lost himself in solicitude over Edith. If he despised himself for this, he couldn't see what else he could have done. If suspicion as well as pain moved in her face, so be it. It was what his life had come to.

Even at ten in the morning there were whores on the ferry. They came off first, singly or in groups, and then gathered, laughing and chatting – a kind of mandatory sociability – in the square before the ferry. Some were provocatively made up; some not made up at all; some were very young, mere girls, some in their forties. Soon sailors joined them, a tight group forming, knit together by bargaining and jokes, the odd sliver of affection. Coming off behind, the other passengers seemed like another caste, circumspect, self-conscious even, going to either side of the first caste. Then, arrangements made, the whores and sailors began to move away.

Taxis were summoned, came forwards. Soon the mass of passengers was moving off as though there hadn't been two castes at all, as though it had been an illusion to suppose so. (An illusion too to imagine, as Douglas had just allowed himself to do, that soon the ferry would be for whores and sailors almost entirely, these being terminal days, base, desperate.)

At first, Douglas couldn't see Helen, and, when he did, he was surprised. She seemed to be moving very slowly, as though, not having seen him for so long, a shyness was upon her. On the windswept gangway she appeared withdrawn. And, seeing her, Douglas felt withdrawn too, uncertain. He wasn't sure whether she was waving or brushing the hair from her eyes, smiling or screwing up her eyes against the bright sun.

When she stepped off the gangway, though, she seemed, like the whores before her, to gain confidence. Spotting Douglas, she smiled broadly, ran forwards.

"Thank God!" Douglas said, holding her. "How good to see you!"

"Such a long time." She spoke calmly, as though, after the embrace, she knew what she hadn't known on the gangway – that the separation hadn't harmed them.

"Too long," Douglas said, embracing her again, touching

her face, tanned from her recent holiday, and her hair, those strong white curls she said she had had since she was twenty.

"It was unavoidable, what with your move and my holiday."

"And how was your holiday? From your letters it seemed all right."

"It was actually."

"You fell in love with Barnie all over again."

"Of course." She laughed, pressing his hand.

Across the square, there was a disturbance: a whore was being ejected from a taxi. She ran after it, shouting, and, when it drew level with Douglas and Helen, threw her handbag at it. The contents spilled, a comb, a packet of tampons, a purse, lipstick, loose change. Covering her face with her hands, she burst into tears, twisting and turning on the spot as if to stop herself from screaming, losing control entirely.

Helen got out of the car to help, squeezing Douglas' hand to keep him where he was, forestall any thoughts he might have that she was making a mistake. Quickly she retrieved the scattered contents and, taking the bag from the girl, replaced them, all the while the girl seeming unaware, lost in distress, twisting. A hand on her shoulder, Helen waited for her to take the bag back, speaking quietly to her, Douglas could see, offering sympathy. She didn't respond at first, but then, suddenly, snatched the bag and walked away, legs awkward and stiffened by high heels, appearing far too young for high heels, crying now as from the difficulty of wearing them.

"Poor lass," Helen said, getting back into the car. "D'you know what I heard on the way over? A girl trying to get it out of a sailor when he was going off to sea. She was crying."

"They're sworn to secrecy, I think."

"I know, but he was making a meal of it, enjoying it."

They sat in silence, holding hands. The whore, strutting now, looking abusive, went out into the road.

"Yes, my holiday. Barnie needs so little now, so very little." She made a nebulous gesture, as of something evaporating.

Ever since Douglas had known her, Helen had referred to her husband, twenty years her senior, as old, in decline, on the way out. At first it hadn't been true – merely a kind of shorthand for their unhappiness, their childlessness, their embarrassment at having married at all. Then it had started to become so. And now it undoubtedly was. One of her jokes had been to stop in the middle of something and pretend to usher Barnie off into death; another to find that he had been dead twenty years and she hadn't noticed. There were no jokes now, however, only pity and forbearance (in which, she said, she had been inspired by Douglas, whose solicitude over Edith had always precluded bitterness and mockery).

"And Edith – how is she?"

"Very tired to start with, in a lot of pain, but better now. And meditating again."

"Oh good."

"We went out on a boat, you see, and had a close up of the base. It seemed to inspire her."

"How d'you mean?"

"To meditate again. A way of coping."

"With the obscenity of it?"

"The horror, yes."

"How do you cope with it?"

"I don't think I do. I don't think I can. Can you?"

"No."

"We experience it but we don't grasp it. The imagination is defeated."

They drove down the main street, but instead of taking the coast road, they took a back road. It wound steeply upwards between pine trees, straightening then and crossing a moor. On the right, after about a mile, there was a high barbed wire fence. Ministry of Defence land. Unpromising, bare and marshy, overlooked by cameras. Between the road and the fence there was a ditch, ten feet deep at least. Douglas had never seen anything happen here, but it was a stretch of road so uncompromisingly straight and with such desolation on either side that he always had the sense that something was about to happen. Hawks hovered or perched on the high fence, wind sang in the wires, and even from the car you could smell bog, the odours of stagnant mud and water, carcasses.

"What a grim stretch," Helen said. "A speed limit too."

"Yes, but I can't understand why. Military officiousness. If I were to put my foot down, we'd be caught by the cameras."

"It gives the moor a chance to work on us."

"Exactly."

Their relationship had had distinct phases, each associated with a place, a landscape. There had been the school in which they met as teachers, the impoverished housing estates surrounding it, one pub serving them all, a pub to which they had sometimes gone after school. There had been the flat near the Botanic Gardens which a friend of Helen's had allowed them to use when she was away on business. In different schools now, they would meet there in the evenings or at weekends, looking down on blossoms and greenery in spring and summer, a river and black suspension bridge in winter. That had gone on for four years, and had been the steadiest time. Next there had been a rented room – their Pakistani landlord referring to them as "my business couple" – in which they had never felt at ease. And now, driving across the moor above the Holy Loch, Douglas felt they were entering another phase, one he would come to associate with this new landscape, a landscape annexed by armies and navies but still so remarkable he sometimes felt he would wake up one day (as though their presence had suddenly been found ridiculous, a folly, a vanity) to find the armies and navies gone.

"I think I'll follow you into retirement here." Helen's voice was low and quiet.

"Good," Douglas said briskly. "Who wants a relationship dependent on ferries?"

They had developed a code for dealing with their hopes and fears, which allowed them to look forwards without mentioning their partners, without seeming to be waiting for their deaths. In their early days, they had spoken openly of what lay in the way of their living together, but as the vanishing of these obstacles had come closer, they had ceased to do so. As if that would have been offensive, sinful. Murderous even. The one time they made an exception, about a year ago, in the rented room, they had had a conversation so bad they were left unable either to speak or to make love. They had had to part for a while. Who was going to die first, Barnie or Edith, and how soon, had been the questions raised, and addressed so boldly they might have been in the habit of waiting for people to die, of hastening their ends even. Ever since, there had been no mention of such matters. Now conversations about their partners had a sort of strained ingenuousness, an ingenuousness born of despair at what lay beyond.

"A good place to retire to. One wouldn't become complacent."

"That's why we chose it, I think. There's no dodging the twentieth century here. And yet it's not without peace."

Across the moor, Douglas turned off the road onto a track which ran into the depths of a wood. He switched off the engine. Total silence. Then, slowly, they became aware of birdsong, now here, now there, now light, now throaty, now in cascades, now in single notes.

The wood was on a hill. They decided to climb to the top, where it was open, views in all directions. Dappled sunlight, birdsong and silence composed the medium in which they moved. They went hand in hand mostly, a picnic basket in Douglas' other hand (he had made the picnic before Edith woke, smuggled it out of the house into the boot of the car). Now and then he squeezed Helen's hand and she, as in renewal of hopes and promises – hopes at least for the day, arranged with such difficulty – squeezed his.

He was glad to see he wasn't breathless, wasn't even monitoring his breathing. Strange notes in the middle of the wood made them pause: not a bird they recognised. Further up, the wood thinned, a breeze fretting its edges. Beyond, there was bright sunlight. They were reluctant to emerge though, to take possession of the hilltop, bare and treeless, conical.

Putting down the basket, Douglas drew Helen towards him. She was smiling. He knew of course that men of his age and with his medical history could die in the act of love. After his heart attack, in fact, he had been advised to wait awhile before "resuming relations". It didn't seem relevant now. His illness was as good as gone, he believed, and might even be said to have strengthened him.

"We've got hours," Helen said, spreading a rug on the ground.

Normally, after separations, they made love uneasily, feeling their way back to each other. Not this time however. Helen cried out joyfully immediately Douglas entered her, tossing her head from side to side, and he, exhilarated, cried out too. It was over more quickly and completely than either could remember. They lay quietly at the edge of the wood, holding one another.

"The seat of the affections," Helen said, a hand on Douglas' chest. "Listen to it go."

"Quite a workout."

"You're not anxious?"

"Not at all. I think, you see, it's only the lustful who die on the job. Die of despair, probably."

"You'll not die then." She spoke gravely, with that touch of self importance he loved in her. "Though you were close to it."

"Too many contradictions, I think. Conflicting impulses translated into the heart, its very rhythms."

"I think that's how it is, you know."

Just before his illness – an early symptom, possibly – he had hardly been able to make love. Each part of himself seemed compromised by some other part, each act shadowed by its opposite. Unaffected immediacy was beyond him, simplicity a memory. When teaching or in company, he had wanted to be alone, when alone, in company. When with Edith, he had longed for Helen, when with Helen, for Edith. His life had ceased to make sense. And directly out of this, as it seemed, had come, one morning, the first of the chest pains.

They straightened their clothes, picked up the basket and went out of the wood towards the hilltop. Here too there had once been trees, they saw, but they had been blasted. Only stumps remained, hollowed out, some dry as bones, others damp and crumbling, a red dust inside. On the summit however, as though opposing itself to the surrounding blight, was a cairn. They stood with their backs to it, looking out over the woods and the moor to the loch beyond. The water was light blue today, but with dark patches, areas of greater depth, Douglas supposed. And very still: no breezes down there.

Douglas became aware that Helen was looking at him.

"Do you see it?" she asked.

"What?"

"The submarine."

While he had been contemplating the loch, Helen had been looking seawards. Following her gaze, Douglas saw the submarine. Intensely black, it was emerging from an area of hazy brightness, a giant fin cleaving the waters, something terrible in its uprightness. For a moment he wasn't sure whether it was returning or leaving; there didn't seem to be any wake. If it was a homecoming, it was a very stealthy one. The hazy brightness then appeared to be coming with it, as though created by it, at once halo and camouflage.

Helen had moved closer and was saying something – what, he didn't hear. He was aware only of her tone, low, perturbed.

Perhaps it was the effect of the light, or of tiredness, Douglas didn't know, but he suddenly had the feeling that there was no mystery to the submarine at all. He was about to be given a glimpse of life on board.

Like rabbits in burrows, they were going to be revealed to him, ordinary men going about ordinary tasks. A disciplined crew, young, courteous and keen, aware for months that they would be at this spot at this time on this day, and that, two months later, say, they would be at it again, sea bound.

A graceful concentration of lines, curves and angles, the submarine then passed out of sight behind the hill, to be guided in by computers, Douglas supposed.

Helen was squeezing his arm to get his attention. Her voice had an edge.

"Surely you've seen one before? Surely?"

"Yes, but not from this angle, and not in this way."

"What do you mean?"

"With such intimacy, the scales falling from my eyes, a close-up."

"Ah."

"Very fanciful, no doubt."

"Not at all."

"Do you …"

"Yes, the same sort of thing," Helen said. "I've seen Barnie in a high chair, an arrested child, leering, demanding food. And on his hands and knees, an old dog looking for a bone or a fuck."

She laughed mirthlessly.

"Not like a dog, do you mean, actually a dog?"

"Yes. And actually in a high chair."

"They could be figments, of course. I'm sure our imaginations get strained, crack a little, mislead us. Who am I to think that submarines are run by young men indistinguishable from one another in their passivity and ordinariness?"

"I like to think it's the best we can do." She spoke stiffly, as if he had been guilty of levity. "Our truest moments."

"Actually I think you're right," he replied. "We have hallucinations, but we also have visions."

She remained a little stiff with him, however. Passionate in her certainties, she didn't take kindly to jokes about them, sceptical insinuations. Once it had bothered him, the solemnity of it, but not now: now what bothered him was that he might appear patronising. He was careful to try and avoid this.

He spread the rug before the cairn and busied himself with the picnic basket, pleased to be able to unpack at leisure what he had prepared surreptitiously at six that morning. Three half bottles of wine, chicken legs, various sandwiches, cheese, fruit, a cake, biscuits, a thermos of coffee. He laid it out on the rug with glasses, plates and cutlery, aware of Helen close behind him, watching at first with curiosity, then with approval.

"I suppose it's along these roads that they march at Easter time," she said.

"That's right."

"Will you march?"

"We can march together."

"Edith?"

"She'd not want to be pushed, I think, on an occasion like that."

He looked into the distance, as in search of other submarines.

But the loch was empty, pale, glittering. Dark clouds had gathered over the sea, far out. As likely to retreat however as advance. He had learnt that much about the weather here.

Late in the afternoon, they drove back to the ferry. In spite of the submarine and a helicopter which, for half an hour or so, had scoured the hills on both sides of the loch, as if looking for someone, they had been happy, at peace. They were calm as they crossed the moor again, the Ministry of Defence territory with its fences, bunkers, ditches, towers and cameras. Calm still when, high up, at a turn in the road, Douglas stopped to point out the base. "Charming," was all Helen said, but lightly, as if she had absorbed the fact of the base into her world view long ago, accounted for it as well as anyone.

Douglas had noted such moods of calm in them before. It was as if they were suddenly granted a break from the world, a holiday, a medium without static or distortion in which to renew themselves. Sacramental interludes. They had come to honour them, knowing they would be brief.

And so it proved. They had to stop for a military vehicle, a lorry with a long covered trailer attached; it had got stuck at one of the bends. And, even then, it wasn't until two men in uniform jumped down from the high cab and, without any kind of explanation, waved them back, further and further back, until they were round the corner and out of sight, that their mood changed. They were outraged. Helen said it was obviously an area in which you were obliged to put up with whatever the military threw at you, Douglas how damned right she was.

Before he could stop her, Helen had grabbed her camera and was out of the car, running, bent double, to the corner. There, squatting, she took snap after snap of the lorry, toppled over in the ditch. Then, bent double again, she ran back, badly out of breath, flushed.

"We can use these in the press," she gasped. "Sell them."

"Why not?" Douglas said. "I can see it. Missile convoy in ditch."

He was already reversing when one of the men from the lorry came round the corner at the double. He was shouting for Helen to give over the camera. "Lady, will you hand that to me please. Lady, haven't you got something you'd like to give me?" Still in reverse, Douglas accelerated violently. The man ran after them for about thirty or forty yards, and seemed to be gaining. Just when it looked as if he was about to catch them though – jump onto the bonnet and pound the windscreen, perhaps – he stopped, dropped to one knee, and began taking snaps in turn. Then he stood up, grinning aggressively, and vanished round the corner.

"If there's such a thing as a NATO file," Douglas said, "that's us in it. Right down to the number plate."

"Who do they think they are? These are public roads, aren't they?"

"Here for our protection, my dear." He hoped she wasn't going to give in to mere complaint. Sometimes she did so, and it could irritate him. "We can't expect our protectors to be nice, can we?"

"Maybe not. But does their role as protectors give them carte blanche?"

"Of course not, but it would be naive not to suspect that they think it does."

"That's obvious; they're so arrogant."

"It's always been so," Douglas said. "Always."

By the time they reached the ferry they were calm again. For some reason, the meeting with the lorry hadn't thrown any shadows. Holding hands, they made their way through the crowd of whores and sailors, their harsh banter, shouted arrangements and goodbyes.

Douglas was still calm, seeing everything very clearly, the screaming gulls, the ferry, turning sturdily in its wake, heading out across the water, the passengers on the upper deck.

Edith's Journal – I

Let me call these jottings. I don't think I've the strength to develop things.

I'm settled here, I think. The pain isn't too bad at the moment, not too bad at all, though that probably means it's gathering itself for an onslaught later, in the winter. I'm grateful though. I can look about me so much more when I'm not in pain. I can see and admire. There's so much to admire.

We went out in a boat the other day. I wasn't aware of any discomfort at all. The nearer to the American base we drifted, actually, the freer I felt. Free of my body. Had we been captured and put in a cell I might have felt freer still. Much to be recommended.

The blessing of self forgetfulness. How awful we need to be shocked into it. Douglas' heart attack and that base. The aim should be to achieve it without such dramas, while sitting on one's own, one's partner out or pottering about. Pain a constant inhibitor though. But precisely that's the challenge. (Imagine it: limbs which are both painful and useless!)

Sometimes when falling asleep I have this image of myself as a ball. My limbs have gone, you see. I roll from room to room, from house to house, a happy attendant spirit, not really a woman any more, I suppose, but does that matter? Isn't wisdom above gender?

The simpler the body, the less the chance of pain. So I'm a little ball when I fall asleep. Why should the spirit need the human body as we know it for its dwelling place? If matter means pain, or the possibility of it, why not simplify matter? Give the spirit a chance, I say.

I'm meditating again, which is the important thing. What with the disorder of the move, I had stopped. Just when I should have kept going. What started me again, I think, was the base. It was horrible. A world in itself. One can imagine other worlds being sucked into it, never to reappear. This is what I do: I sit in the bay window of the lounge and gaze at some pine trees. After a while, if the light and my mood are right, I find a place in the greeny darkness. And then I seem able to move downwards, towards a promise of light. I don't will myself downwards; I'm drawn. Afterwards, I'm so refreshed. I avoid thinking about the base though. How can one think about it anyway? It's unthinkable. All we can do is diminish it by having higher thoughts. The hope must be that one day it'll have no place.

I'd really thought that we were going to be two invalids together, Douglas with his heart trouble, me with this. I'd even thought I mightn't die first after all. He'd become stooped and hesitant and his colour was bad. But he's better now. And being so nice to me, though sometimes I can spot the effort it costs him. Poor Douglas. To have to dress and undress a sixty year old woman whose body has gone, do all the shopping and all the cooking. On the whole he does it very well, almost gallantly. His touch is kind, so that some-times I get a little thrill when he's dressing or undressing me. I don't let him suspect it though. What would be the point? There are things better left unsaid.

Today he's gone to Glasgow to see his solicitor and have lunch with friends. He was eager to be off, I could see that, and I glad to let him go. An empty house is best for a jour-nal – whatever this is – and meditation. We'll be the better for it. He'll have news for me tonight and I, well, news of a kind for him.

IV

Driving to the ferry to meet his son, Larry, Douglas found himself thinking, not for the first time either, that Edith and he could have been luckier with their only child. It seemed he only came home when he was unhappy. Two years ago it had been a broken love affair; now it was "a sudden redundancy".

He had the thought with affection though. In one sense only could they have been luckier, and that a trivial one; in another, deeper sense luck consisted in having a child at all. Their home was his home, and after they had died it would – if he wanted it, could stand the isolation – be his home still. There had been a time, however, just before his illness, when Larry's waywardness had enraged Douglas. But these rages, as though part of the illness, early symptoms, had gone. He was left with a sense of space that was at once physical and spiritual. It allowed him to regard his son less personally – a child of the late twentieth century rather than simply of his parents. The silences between generations: he had learnt to accept them, not to fill them with tendentious talk.

It was the same ferry he had met Helen off three weeks before. On a misty day with drizzle, fog horns sounding, he didn't see it until it had almost docked. Its lights lit up the pier, the groups of whores and sailors sheltering under umbrellas. First off as usual, other whores and sailors came down the gangway. For some moments all Douglas could hear were male American voices marshalling the whores, ordering them here, ordering them there.

The remaining passengers followed after what might

have been seen as a decent interval. Or so it seemed to Douglas, sheltering under his own umbrella, looking out for his son.

Larry was at the back, looking about him with a kind of ostentatious curiosity. Typical of him, Douglas thought. How he took his time on such occasions. Whether coming off ships or walking along platforms, he took his time, managed to give the impression that he was the first to have observed these places faithfully. It went with his inability or refusal to give you his full attention, Douglas felt. Charming in his unselfconscious youth, but now an irritation. Douglas had to work hard not to show it. It wasn't easy. Seeing him again after so many months, for instance, wasn't it the first thing he noticed?

That and the largeness of his head. A big head, with straight sandy hair. Quite a thin neck though: almost feminine. Not that these features irritated him as the dilatoriness did. On the contrary, they made him smile and move forwards, start to wave.

They shook hands, Douglas still with the vision of Larry's large head and sandy hair, Larry not seeming to be responsive to anything in his father at all, but looking about him again, at the whores especially, their outrageous seductiveness.

"Are they here all the time?"

Speaking slowly, as though to combat his son's excitability, Douglas replied that he had never been to the pier.

"Wherever there are soldiers or sailors there will be whores," Larry said. "War means business."

"War is business," Douglas said, now also looking about him.

"Fancy any of them?" Larry smiled.

"On my day, all of them." He smiled too: a joke for his son.

For some reason he felt that Larry had lost the power to unsettle him, a development for which he was grateful.

43

Still smiling, he said he supposed it was always possible to find someone to fancy. Our needs were such that someone could always be found to fit the bill, whatever that was. Didn't Larry agree? He asked even although he knew that his son had not had much success with women, and even although he suspected that, behind "the sudden redundancy", there was another sad story. Edith would probably be told about it before he was, and it would be she who told him then, not Larry.

"Without his fancies, a man is barren," Larry said, picking up his suitcase and making for the car.

Douglas remembered this too: the throwaway maxim that was supposed to stop you in your tracks.

Larry couldn't make up his mind whether to put his suitcase in the back of the car or in the boot, and made more of it than he need have done. Then he put it down and forgot about it, for a quarrel had broken out between two whores.

It was still drizzling, but Douglas felt no inclination to hurry his son. Perhaps in retirement he had learnt patience. After his illness, a more reflective pace. He wondered if Larry would notice.

"What do you think they're quarrelling about?" Larry pointed at the whores, as if it wasn't obvious who he was referring to. "At this time in the morning?"

Douglas shrugged his shoulders, hoping Larry would get into the car. But he didn't. Instead, hands on hips, he sidled up to the whores like a schoolboy trying to impress his mates. This sort of thing also Douglas remembered: the excruciating miscalculation, insolence backfiring. He wondered if Larry would have done it had he been on his own. Playing to the gallery. It had been in his school reports.

Caught up by a whores' quarrel. Down to the last detail Douglas could see what was going to happen, so that, when it did – the whores breaking off from each other and turning on Larry as though to rend him – he had a sense of his son as fated. Perversity and mischance. Vexed, he watched as he came back, a slightly shambling gait, shoulders hunched, head rolling.

"Curiosity isn't appreciated these days," Larry said, getting into the car.

"There are better things to be curious about around here." It might help, he thought, if he could interest his son in more important matters. His voice was earnest. "The submarine base, for example, the comings and goings, the strange noises at four in the morning. It's at four in the morning, actually, that I think the world will end."

"Probably." Larry seemed suddenly exhausted. "Whores and the rest of us together."

"Look at this, for instance," Douglas said. "A very familiar scene on the roads around here. Nonetheless threatening though. Time and again one is compelled to witness it."

Jack-knifed at the crossroads just outside the ferry terminal was a huge military transport. A crowd had gathered to watch as, helped by two policemen, the driver tried to extricate himself. But wherever he moved, left or right, backwards or forwards, he had to come back to where he had started, and, each time he did so, the crowd jeered.

"There will be missiles on board," Douglas said.

Larry had a hand under his chin, as though to support his head. His head was nodding slightly. Douglas couldn't tell whether he was paying attention to the scene or not.

"They will have come up from southern England," he continued. "The routes are carefully chosen, and vary."

Certainly, he thought, he must help his son to move beyond idle curiosity. It was imperative he learned concentration. A sober eye for the dark event. Poise, collectedness. Sitting beside him, aware of his restlessness, he formulated it all quite consciously. A project for his declining years. Coda to his earnestness. He laid a hand on Larry's arm, nodding at the scene before them.

"The traditional colour for camouflage – mottled dark green. But it looks wrong in the main street of a small town, doesn't it?"

Larry licked his lips before replying, as if to increase his chances of speaking clearly.

"The feeling I have with these military guys is that, although they're engaged in something deadly serious, it's really a game to them."

"Exactly. And it has to be, otherwise they'd not be able to do it at all."

"Which means they're actually unfit for it."

"Yes. That's why the players are either never seen at all or seen only rarely."

"How do you mean?"

"Well, recently," Douglas said, eager to tell his son this, "I saw a submarine. It was returning from one of its trips. It was very black. A black submarine on a beautiful day. For a moment or two I fell into a kind of trance. It was as if I had x-ray eyes; I seemed to see right into it. I could see the crew going about their business. They were very ordinary young men – very ordinary indeed – but what struck me especially was that they and their tasks … had their backs to each other."

"An agreement not to see … ?"

"I think so. It'll be part of the training."

"I must say … it's some place you've chosen to retire to," Larry said after a pause. "I admire you for it."

"Well, you know us: eager to be in the thick of it."

"And how are you both? Mother?"

"Holding her own. Remarkable really."

"And you? You're looking well."

"I am. Most days I feel completely recovered."

At last they were able to follow the military transport out of the town. Douglas' windscreen wipers were on, drowning out the sound of the transport as, in low gear, it negotiated the bends of the coast road. Always about two bends ahead, it appeared to move with more purpose than any of the vehicles behind, appeared to confer on them a kind of futility, in fact, so that after a bit Douglas felt it would be a mistake to go any closer. He was sitting pressed well back in his seat and out of the corner of his eye he saw that Larry was sitting that way too.

"Talk about setting the pace," Larry said.

"Don't worry; we're close to the turn-off."

Because of the thick mist Douglas didn't stop to show Larry the base, as he had planned to. Larry was quiet now, as quiet as he had been talkative. It was always so before reunions with his mother. And it would be the same, Douglas knew, for Edith, waiting in the cottage. A deeply uneasy quietness. In recent years their reunions had been so fiercely emotional he had left them to it. Something in them he couldn't bear. The son, weeping with relief and gratitude, bending low over his mother, the mother, pale and wasted, clasping the son to her with what strength she could summon. There was no place for a third person, even although that third person bore witness to their reunion with a kind of grief. And he was powerless to calm them then. Only the son could calm the mother, the mother the son.

They found that Edith, having wheeled herself down the garden path, was fumbling with the aluminium catch of the gate. Through the still air the sound came over clearly. Douglas stopped by the car while Larry hurried over, waving and calling as he went. The fumbling became frantic. Douglas thought he could hear his wife cursing (certainly he could imagine the half dead fingers defeated by the latch), then crying, a crying which briefly became ecstatically welcoming before sinking to a kind of keening or lamentation.

He busied himself with Larry's case, shut the boot twice, his own door and the passenger door once each. He walked a little way with the case before looking up and seeing

Larry bent over the wheelchair in the garden. The gate was open, the ramp which went down from it glistening in the drizzle. He went on slowly, hoping that by the time he reached the gate Larry would be pushing his mother back up the garden towards the cottage.

The gate was only about eighty yards from the car but, as in a dream, it took Douglas a long time to reach it. He didn't think he had ever moved in such a grave and measured way. His thoughts were peculiar also, to do, it seemed, with emotion, its character, significance. Larry bent over his mother in the wheelchair in the garden, frieze of the family's troubled heart. But what were they for, these emotions, what did they mean? How did they leave you, once they had passed? Defeated, advanced? Degraded, elevated? Were there emotions which revealed, which penetrated appearances to lay bare the truth behind, and emotions which obscured, confused, misled? How tell the one from the other?

Then he found that he had arrived at the gate and that his hand was on his son's back. Larry, smiling weakly, was trying to work out how to turn the wheelchair. Edith was making sounds, but they weren't words. Douglas reached down to the black knob of the brake and pulled it. Then, bending low, he pushed the wheelchair up the garden path. The drizzle had become rain, Edith's collar was soaked, stuck to her neck, and her hair was plastered to her skull. He reached dawn to touch her, to wipe away the rain, drawn painfully to the shape of the skull, so rarely seen. Could emotion excite emotion, he wondered, his own set free, by the fearful closeness between mother and son, to range into the past? He wasn't sure, but the image he had was a simple one, of Edith's head, hair plastered to her skull as now, being held in his hands. Twenty years ago probably. Maybe more.

"At least it's warm today," he said.

The cottage delighted Larry, and taking one of his mother's hands in his, he said so.

"Why didn't you tell me? Why didn't you make it clearer what it was like?"

Some of Edith's strictness had returned.

"We did. We sent you photographs. You can't have paid them much attention."

"They didn't do it justice."

"Or you didn't do them justice. Perhaps you were distracted."

"Perhaps."

She followed him with her eyes as he walked about the lounge. This was the next stage, Douglas remembered: after the delirium of reunion, Larry seen soberly, and Larry behaving as if he had been in his mother's company for weeks, even showing signs of finding it uncomfortable. So much given, so much feared, such advances and retreats.

"You've certainly landed on your feet," Larry said, raising his hands in little gestures of recognition whenever he saw familiar furniture.

"In my case, perhaps you could rephrase that," his mother said.

She fell silent then. Douglas was silent too. He wasn't sure of the reasons for her silence, but thought he understood the reasons for his own. Larry hadn't come when he had his heart attack, hadn't come when they moved house. He only brought them his disasters, the aftermath of his defeats. And made little attempt to conceal it. Douglas couldn't remember one simple visit, and, suddenly, it shocked him.

"I hope you're going to make yourself useful," Edith said. "There's a lot to do in the cottage and in the garden. If it's therapy you're after, the garden will provide it. But you're most welcome, of course …"

Some asperity or evasiveness in her manner must have struck Larry as he was about to leave the lounge, for he turned suddenly and sat down. Hands clasped between his knees, he made as though to speak. Edith was wheeling herself towards him.

49

"Well my dear," she said, "what is it this time? What has brought you so low in the November of this year?"

By a slight raising of the eyebrows Edith indicated that she didn't want Douglas to leave the room. He sat down and folded his arms. Larry was still making as if to speak, still failing to do so. Once or twice he looked up at his parents and smiled uncertainly. In the silence – on the edges of which the rain was now falling steadily – he seemed, Douglas thought, exactly what he was – a disturbed and unhappy young man. Nailed by his mother's strictness, held by her questions, he looked at last to Douglas. Douglas didn't respond, not because he felt no pity, but because, for the moment, he felt more curiosity than pity.

As the minutes passed, it was as if the helplessness of the son grew in proportion to the curiosity of the father, the curiosity and exasperation of the mother. Douglas reflected that each time Larry had come home, his reasons had been darker. First, he had failed some exams; second, he had failed the resits; third, he had lost his licence for drunk driving; fourth, he had got a girl pregnant and needed money for an abortion.

"Is it trouble with the police?" Douglas asked.

Larry appeared to shake his head.

"Maybe you're going to have to fall very low before you can rise," Edith said, watching him closely.

Larry laughed, a high, strangled sound.

"You seem to have persuaded yourselves you've got a criminal before you."

"It's our son before us," Edith said quietly, "our son who always comes like a thief in the night."

"As bad as that?" He was scratching his head as in an attempt to find a way of dealing with his parents. "Really?"

"You fly to us rather than come to us," Douglas said, more indulgently than he had intended. "We'll always be here, of course, but … should a young man be quite so often in need of sanctuary?"

"Point taken," Larry mumbled. "A sanctuary on the Holy Loch."

"Call it what you like," Edith said, "you can't stay here and not come clean."

"Come clean?" Larry responded, as if the words were barely intelligible. "Come clean?"

He threw his right foot onto his left knee and clasped it at the ankle with both hands.

"As good a time as any, don't you think?" Unusual tension in his neck and chest, Douglas had set himself to breathe deeply.

Larry said something about his parents speaking with one voice – a slightly biblical one at that – laughed, fell silent again. Edith wheeled herself over to the window and looked out. Douglas went to the kitchen, where, after a few moments, he fancied he heard sobbing, mother and son collapsing again, another paroxysm. But he knew it couldn't be so; Edith would never let herself go twice in one day.

He returned to the lounge with the tea tray. Neither Edith nor Larry had moved. Once the tea had been poured, however, Larry said that, if they would bear with him, he would explain himself, or, since he wasn't entirely sure what had happened, try to do so.

"I think I've always tried to get on in the world," he began, his voice unsteady, his hands describing vague shapes, his head, as though unusually burdened, held to one side. "I've always felt I owed it to myself, and to you, to do so. And so it'll remain, I'm sure. Why play safe? Why be a spectator? The world is for participants, not spectators. It's participants who make it what it is. But my way of participating seems to be unfortunate, to say the least. It's taken me some time to realise it, which is unfortunate too. I've kidded myself I can go it alone, daringly and decisively, that I don't need others. But actually I'm on the lookout for allies all the time. All the bloody time!"

For the first time since sitting down, he leant back. It was as if he had at last seen how he might account for himself. He looked at his parents, but, as though to keep their concentration, they didn't look back.

"Yes, it seems I'll go to any lengths to get allies. I think my disasters have a pattern. In search of allies, intimates, I overreach myself. I don't think I'm careless about right and wrong, but when it comes to winning a friend, securing an ally, I become prone ... to a kind of cheating. It's as if, when the crunch comes and an ally is there to be won or lost, I'm prepared to do anything. And for a time I can persuade myself it's not wrong! This last episode, for instance. Well, let me tell you about it. Don't spare me: nothing to be gained by that, I think you'll agree."

A wind had risen, blowing rain against the windows. A shutter creaked and a door banged, but Douglas and Edith, as though trying to imagine the worst that Larry could tell them, didn't stir.

"We were planting a fir forest in Northumberland. It meant staying in caravans for two months. John Livingston, our supervisor, thought he'd invite his wife down, because the weather was so good and they'd not had a holiday. She came, but she wasn't particularly amused. John was away all day, you see, working on drainage, and when he came back in the evenings he was exhausted. Although my caravan was quite a bit away from theirs, I could hear them arguing each night. Actually, I could see them arguing, for if you have a heated argument in a caravan, the caravan shakes."

He paused, smiled a little, then continued.

"At the end of the first week, John asked me and another of the workers, Peter Paterson, if we'd like to have a meal with him and his wife. We agreed because, well, there's nothing to do in these places. The caravan was barely big enough for the four of us, though with the door open and the night warm, it wasn't too bad. Janet, John's wife, had gone to a lot of trouble. She had a pink dress on, pink with white spots, and I thought, I thought, how odd to dress like that in a caravan. After the meal, we played cards until, around midnight, Janet said she'd had enough. Peter and John then brought up the problem of the drainage again – it hadn't been fixed, you see. Ten minutes of that and Janet jumped up and said she was going for a walk. For some reason, she wanted me to go too. She was exasperated with her husband and she'd not taken to Peter. Not that I want to suggest she'd taken a fancy to me – not at that stage anyway. Now here's the funny thing: I knew I shouldn't go with her. Even although John made a joke of it, saying it was quite all right, I knew it wasn't, absolutely knew it! I knew it as I know … you don't lift a melon from a stall and go off without paying for it."

He had been speaking with increasing animation, but suddenly he shrugged his shoulders, spread his hands, and seemed to appeal to his parents. When he spoke again – as out of a dream of confusion and defeat – it was in a low voice. A helicopter passing over the cottage obliged him to pause, then speak loudly, his voice rising against the blows of engine noise striking the sides of the cottage.

"I'm sure you can imagine what happened. Janet quickly got it into her head that I was superior to her husband. A superior companion, more knowledgeable about trees and forests and drainage, and, she was soon implying, probably a better lover too. She even insinuated that if I played my cards correctly, I might get her husband's job. It was just a matter of waiting.

She knew things about her husband, she hinted, that would be to my advantage. Well, we went around together for a few weeks, apparently with John's approval. He'd have done anything to keep her quiet, you see, to stop her from complaining."

He paused again, grimacing, as the helicopter came back over the cottage.

"Then a most unfortunate thing happened. We'd arranged to meet in town, but before going there I was to collect some extra money from their caravan. She didn't like carrying a lot on her. It wasn't where she said it would be, however, in an inside pocket of a brown jacket she sometimes wore, so I looked for it elsewhere. That was in John's clothes as well as hers. What else was I to do? But I was caught in the act: the caravan door opened and John came in. I hadn't heard him coming. In fact, I was under the impression that he was working late. He accused me of theft. I denied it and tried to explain myself, but he laughed in my face. I punched him. We had a fight then, all over the caravan. Later, when I asked Janet to confirm my story, she wouldn't. She said it looked like theft to her too. That made me wonder … wonder if I had been set up. I'm pretty sure I was."

When he spoke again it was more painfully than before.

"It brought them together again. Can you believe it? The caravan didn't shake any more – at least, not from their rows. And I … I was fired. Any protests and I'd have been charged with theft. That was made clear. So here I am."

As if he didn't believe that after such a confession either of his parents could possibly have much to say to him, Larry got up, suddenly and quietly, and left the room. They saw him in the garden then – as though to avoid seeming pathetic, looking up at the helicopter.

Douglas went out into the garden after him. They watched the helicopter together.

"There are times when I take their noise and presence almost personally," Douglas said.

"I've heard that they sometimes use isolated cottages as reference points in their manoeuvres."

"I wouldn't be surprised; it often seems so."

"A terrible noise. I could hardly hear myself speak in there."

"You spoke very well, very well indeed." The wretchedness of what Larry had said had affected him less, Douglas found, than the honesty of the telling. "I appreciated it, and so did your mother. It can't have been easy."

Larry shrugged his shoulders.

"Would you mind if I stayed a while? A month, maybe more?"

"As long as you like."

Because Larry wouldn't look at him, Douglas laid a hand on his shoulder. Inside, Edith had put on some lights; they seemed to beckon to her family to come back in. This they did when, as though suddenly summoned, the helicopter banked off towards the north.

Edith's Journal – II

Larry is home again. The thought never quite leaves me that one day he'll be home for good. Is this the time? He seems more hurt and lost than ever. A few times I've caught myself whispering "my boy". A bad sign. Larry is twenty-five. After an opening confession which moved us both very much, he's been very silent. I try to let him be. So does Douglas, but he's better at it than I. I have a tendency to probe, to make pointed enquiries. The way he looks up when I make them, his big head turning slowly and wearily, I'm instantly ashamed. But I don't want him to think that we're not concerned.

I don't want him to get the idea that his crises over the years have wearied us. There are punch drunk parents, I know, parents who can't take any more, but that's not us. Douglas says it's a matter of faith, of having faith in his faith in us. Yes, faith in his faith. What if life is finally a network of such faiths? The ultimate bedrock? That or nothing at all?

My health has been bad again. The pain came back not long after Larry's return (there's no connection, of course).

Always the return of bad pain is like a renewal of hostilities. Always, to start with, it's as if there's someone behind it, directing it. For a few days I personify it, only knowing my attitude is right when I stop doing this, when I understand again that pain is impersonal, mindless, random.

I've stepped up my painkillers, three three times a day instead of just two. My days are rather drugged, as a result; I find it hard to get going. Sometimes I can't see the end of my sentences; I tail off. Douglas is very patient with me though. He adjusts his pace to mine, speaking more slowly, pausing when I need a rest, never letting me feel he's got something better to do (though I'm sure he has). What I hate most is the feeling of passivity. I can't be bothered asserting myself. I'm content just to be nursed. I barely talk, and Douglas' and Larry's conversations, such as they are, I follow from a tired distance, if I follow at all. And this journal: I think it would be beyond me if it wasn't that the chance to keep it … well, let me just say that though the pain makes it hard to keep, keeping it gives me strength.

Would more pain make for more initiative? Maybe. So hard to strike a balance. Too drugged or too much in pain. Is there a state in between – alertness threatened by pain but not eclipsed? Doctor Macfarlane is coming tomorrow so I'll ask him. I'll ask about Larry too, for he's not eating or sleeping well. Sometimes I see him belching into the back of his hand, then drawing in his cheeks strangely, as if he's in pain as well.

I've not let on that the pain is worse, of course. From the way he looks at me, though, I can see that Douglas suspects. I'm quite devious really, only taking two pills if he's around, swallowing the third later. What's to be gained by frankness in these matters, if you come to think of it? What's wrong with courageous deception? I know this is an age for confidences, sharing, counselling, but I think that there are times when sharing is neither possible nor desirable. Funnily enough, I think Douglas is also holding back, not telling me things, worries about his heart especially. And Larry certainly is: I can see it in his eyes, the set of his shoulders, I can hear it in his whistling. If there's love in the family at all – and I think there is – it's what's making it possible for us to behave like this. It's as if we all know it, and as if knowing it enables us to continue with the tender masquerade. I mean, if Douglas and Larry were ignorant of the pain I have to endure, would I be so concerned to keep it to myself?

Should it not be possible, anyway, to use our pain in some way? Were the endeavours of the saints not fuelled by suffering and mortification? I've been thinking a lot about this recently. What my particular endeavour will be, I don't know, but I have faith that it'll be revealed to me, as I have faith that my pain will drive me forth and inspire me when the time comes.

I'm as secretive about this, however, as I am about the fact that my pain has come back and that I don't think it will go away again this time.

V

In spite of his troubled state, Larry quickly took his place in the family again. His parents allowed him to come and go as he pleased. Afraid that questions would drive him away again or cause him to crack up altogether, they respected his whims and silences, Douglas in particular at pains to act as if his behaviour was quite normal really. He believed that it would relax him, help him to come round in time.

But it wasn't always easy to see him as normal. Sometimes he would come in late and watch television in his room until six in the morning; sometimes pace up and down in the garden, a glass of vodka in his hand, talking to himself; sometimes get up at noon, have breakfast, then go back to bed; sometimes, for half an hour or so, play his music extraordinarily loudly. Edith's inclination was to discuss such behaviour and gently discourage it, but Douglas persuaded her not to. So there were days when little was said, their three lives, intensely separate, giving rise to three different kinds or qualities of silence in the cottage.

Occasionally Larry would take the car when he went out, but if he thought he was going to be drinking – and usually he thought this – he would walk down the hill and catch a bus. There was no pattern to his outings, so far as Douglas could see; they appeared wholly random. Once or twice he hinted that he'd like to come along too, for a change of scene, lunch in the Eagle Inn, maybe, or in The Haven, further along the coast, but Larry didn't respond. And whenever Edith and he were going for a run, they would ask Larry if he wanted to join them. He always declined, as appreciative of the empty cottage, apparently, as he was of leaving it when his parents were there.

Once he asked Douglas if he could come with him to the town. He had business there, he said. Douglas dropped him at the drinking fountain in the town square, doing so casually, as though it was a regular occurrence, as though his son's ways were transparently simple and worthy, not obscure and unexplained. In the rear-view mirror he saw him fold his arms and wait by the fountain nonchalantly.

He would always see him off, asking if he had enough money, would be back late, might need to be picked up from somewhere. Because Edith couldn't easily get to the front door, he felt that the rituals of departure and return were his to sustain. He was very particular about them, hating casualness. But Larry was indifferent to such rituals. Douglas persisted nonetheless, having faith that in time and probably without Larry ever knowing it they would bear fruit.

On the little hill which rose behind the back garden Douglas built a hut for his telescope. At chest level there was a bench on which the telescope stood, and from the bench to the roof for three hundred and sixty degrees the hut was open to the skies. It didn't matter that there was barely enough room to stand up in because, when he got excited, Douglas tended to crouch at the telescope. He called it his "observatory", though he suspected Larry was right when he said it looked more like an outside lavatory. It was surrounded by gorse bushes, and quickly became a haunt for birds, even big ones, like crows and seagulls. It gave Douglas pleasure to think that when he wasn't using it, the birds were. He covered the floor with cardboard and newspapers, replacing them every week or so.

Sometimes in the winter darkness he stayed in the hut for as long as three hours, coming down at midnight or later. He wore an overcoat, gloves and a scarf, and on especially cold nights took up a flask of tea as well. Outside the cottage there were trees, some tall ones, but here his view was uninterrupted. It was the best observatory he had ever had; he was determined to make full use of it in the time remaining. Some nights, leaving Edith in front of the television, or in bed, he would climb the hill slowly, feeling, for some reason, that this time might be short. His heart seemed all right again, he wasn't breathless, even felt quite vital, but he had the feeling nonetheless. After using the telescope for an hour or so, however, the feeling would be gone. The heavens restored him. It was close to what he sometimes felt with Helen: their passion seemed able to defeat time, carry some kind of guarantee of indefinite survival.

One night in late January, having helped Edith to bed after dinner (had the worst of the pain come back, that she should be so tired?), and having seen Larry off to town (he had "friends" to see), Douglas climbed to his observatory through a keen wind. The spread of stars exhilarated him. So much remained mysterious in each quarter of the heavens. The naked eye saw a fraction of what existed, and what it saw was not as it was but as it had been millennia ago. He would always start with such simple truths, lingering outside the hut to ponder them. To renew his amazement was essential: otherwise he couldn't enter the hut at all, put his eye to the telescope, look upwards.

It was a good time of the year for Gemini. It was high in the sky and due south, with Orion the hunter lower and south west. Lower still was Canis Minor with the star Procyon, lower again Canis Major with Sirius, amongst the brightest of all the stars. Then, from south south east to north north west, there was the Milky Way, its arch embracing Gemini and Orion, its highest point Capella in Auriga.

To trace the course of the Milky Way was to risk a kind of vertigo, he knew. Nothing on earth affected him comparably. To skim over star clusters, vast areas of space, was dangerous. To avoid feeling as though he was being drawn upwards, spinning through an ever opening funnel, he had to know which part of the sky he was going to study. Space had to be approached with a plan and in a spirit of earnest enquiry if it wasn't to overwhelm you. Yet if he put his eye to the telescope just to confirm what he already knew, he would quickly feel the weight of what he didn't know. The course was a challenging one, between caution and abandon, the penalties for failing quite severe. He recalled a time when for hours after leaving the telescope he had felt that the earth was tilting beneath him, clear and familiar objects sliding out of reach; a time when he had had to sit in a chair, fearful that if he were to rise and open the front door he would be swept away by interstellar gales. (You could hear these sometimes, he fancied, dark sounds, weird sounds, constant background to astonishing splendour.)

In the months before his heart attack, when he had felt low and tired most of the time, he had been particularly aware of his relationship with the stars. Three good nights at the telescope and he would be refreshed and in equilibrium, three bad ones and he would feel done for. One of the strangest thoughts he had now was that the heart attack could have been prevented altogether had he immersed himself in the stars more ardently and imaginatively, not allowed his relationship with them to be coloured by his condition, the unsteadiness of his heart.

For some time after his illness he didn't touch the telescope. He would dream of the stars, though, he would imagine what he would see and feel when he returned to them. When it happened, the return was remarkable. One night, impulsively, with the beginnings of joy, he set up the telescope in the attic of his old house and drew open the skylight. The diffuse yellowness of the city night was almost eclipsed by a fierce overarching darkness. He found himself in a part of the sky he didn't recognise at first, a cluster of extraordinarily bright stars. Only slowly did he realise that it was a constellation in the Crab Nebula long familiar to him. It glittered like a necklace on dark velvet, stars in radiant colloquy, inviting, he believed, a kind of adoring contemplation. It had never appeared so before, and it made him think that his illness might have changed him, that he was coming at the world differently. (How differently, he believed the heavens themselves would show him.)

The conditions tonight were perfect. There was no distorting urban glow, only the deep darkness of the countryside. Had they gone to live by the shore, he would have been troubled by the noise and glare of the American base, but, up here, in the intense cold darkness, the approach to the stars was direct, pure. He would stay at the telescope until his hands were numb and his eyes watered. Then, back in the cottage, he would probably think again of ways of heating the observatory, for in his later years, he believed, he would be spending more and more time there. How strange the sense that critical passions awaited him, times of reckoning. It made him grasp the telescope boldly, almost as if – the observer observed – it was to be trained inwards as well as outwards.

He was cold, but he couldn't break off from Gemini. He might have observed it for much longer, he thought, flirted with the illusion that Sirius was bright enough to command his attention until dawn, but on some far periphery of consciousness he heard a car door slam and his son laugh in the darkness. Trying to keep pace with a female laugh apparently. Competitive but yearning to be close. Douglas stood up, head spinning, and began to take down the telescope. It was what a friend called the period of re-entry. You were never quite sure you'd make it. All these galactic wastes might have done for you. Between heaven and earth confounded. He stepped outside the hut and banged his gloved hands together, swung his arms and stamped his feet. In the moonlight he could see his breath and his watch. Two a.m. Now that Larry and his friend or friends had gone indoors, there was silence again. Looking at the stars, you ceased to be aware of earthly silence. It was something else you sensed, a kind of cosmic lull in which all matter was involved. Now again Douglas knew the silence of the night, relished it as if it contained antidotes for instability. He breathed very deliberately for a few moments, before, cautiously, as if the path was treacherous, starting down to the cottage. Lights were on now, and he thought he heard laughter again.

He was pleased that Larry had found some companions, but he didn't want to risk his mood of calm with the young. Especially with new acquaintances, Larry had a way of playing the cynic, the leveller, that could antagonise. He went in by the back door and tiptoed towards the bedroom in which, he hoped, Edith had been asleep for hours. The lounge door opened abruptly, however, and Larry stepped out, standing in a shaft of light and beckoning. Head lowered, Douglas went down the corridor towards him, aware that his son was swaying slightly, but less troubled by this than he was by the atmosphere of forced gaiety in the room behind.

"Come and meet Ruth and Robert," Larry said, putting a hand on his father's shoulder. "I've been telling them about you."

"Just for a moment then. It's very late."

"The night is young," Larry said, not so much to his father as to his companions.

To cover himself as he adjusted to the light and the visitors, Douglas started to speak, his voice excited, as if he had a tale to tell and this was the moment to tell it. He didn't bother to sit down, but stood in the middle of the lounge, hands clasped by his chest.

"How d'you do? This is the clearest night we've had in months, since my wife and I came here, in fact. For some of my fellow astronomers, you know, it's a matter of life and death to have such skies. Without them, they're not just shut off from the stars, they're shut off from themselves. They pine. I've not quite reached that stage, but I can imagine it. So long live clear skies! Yes, Larry, a cup of tea would be very welcome; I've been up there for hours and I'm pretty cold."

Larry and his companions stood smiling and swaying during this speech. Ruth's face, beneath a mass of brown curls, was neat but pretty, and her hand, when at last she was able to offer it to Douglas, was neat too and jingling with bracelets. Robert was tall, with short hair, very clear eyes and an earnest face. Even before he spoke, saying "Pleased to meet you, sir", Douglas knew he was American. He held himself in a disciplined way, shook hands very correctly, as if entering a contract of some kind, and then would not sit down until Douglas had done so. Ruth was not so formal, drawing her legs under her after she sat and, as if to massage her scalp, burrowing her fingers into her hair.

"You've had a pleasant evening?" Douglas asked.

"Yes," Ruth said. "We met your son in the American club. He bought us drinks and we got talking. He'd been to see a girl called Yvonne, but that …"

"That was only because I owed her money!" Larry seemed delighted to be able to admit it. "I borrowed a fiver from her last week for a taxi."

"Everyone owes Yvonne money," Robert said. "Even I do."

"Even you do?" Ruth said, laying a hand on his knee. "How come?"

"How come? Because she's loaded."

All three laughed, Larry then adding that as well as being loaded, Yvonne was a major-general's daughter, always at a loose end.

Douglas hadn't been able to imagine what Larry did when he went out. He never said, didn't even drop hints, and Douglas never asked. If the main reason for this was a wish not to seem nosey, there was another one: he dreaded to discover that his son's social life was on the desperate side. But now, calm and clear-sighted after his hours with Gemini, this was precisely how it struck him. The club, the casual debts, the drinking, the unnecessary taxi rides. Above all, this couple, Robert and Ruth, Larry so obviously interested in Ruth, Ruth, equally obviously, with no interest in him at all. When he handed her a glass of wine, for instance, he did so pointedly, lingeringly, as if the moment had unusual significance and he was just waiting for her to see it. Back in his chair, he seemed to investigate the boniness of his head, as if suspecting it might be more of a drawback than he had thought. Ruth busied herself with her hair. Holding up her left hand with all fingers spread, she plunged it into her curls, at first as if to scratch her scalp merely, then as if to rearrange her hair in some way, finally however drawing out single hairs and playing with them, teasing them out between thumb and forefinger. While doing so, her gaze went blank – a kind of narcissistic trance, Douglas thought. He felt sorry for his son, trying so hard to impress the young lady with witticisms. The trouble was, they weren't witticisms. Calmly then, the mood in which he had left the telescope undisturbed even by Larry's embarrassing awkwardness – the young people seen as from a distance indeed – Douglas decided to intervene. He turned to Robert, his manner alert, decisive.

"And how d'you find Scotland?"

"Well, sir, each time I write home I say it's the most beautiful country in the world. That about sums up my feelings."

"But what about us, the Scots? We mustn't be confused with the landscape."

"Absolutely worthy of the landscape, sir."

Now that Robert was talking, Ruth was paying attention, hands out of her hair and in her lap, folded there.

"In spite of a certain resistance to your presence here, you find us so?"

"Certainly, sir. You're not guilty of letting politics get in the way of hospitality."

"For some of us, I'd like to say, your presence is desirable," Ruth said.

"Are you speaking personally or politically?" Douglas asked.

"Both actually," Ruth said, smiling.

"My point is, sir, that whether people want our bases or not, they're invariably pleasant to us."

"But should they be?" Douglas asked, beginning to feel that Robert's words were prepared ones, learned from some kind of handbook for naval officers. "Is it a virtue on our part?"

"I beg your pardon?"

"I mean, should we be invariably pleasant to you?" He smiled as he asked it.

"I don't think that's for me to say, sir."

"Why not? It's a simple question about morals."

"Morals? Oh I see ..."

Douglas had noted before that officers in the armed forces addressed you as if they were standing to attention. He wondered if Robert's extreme pleasantness, democratic manners, were part of an attempt to bring him to attention too. Respect before the flag. Duty. He shifted in his seat, leant forwards.

"I can hardly believe you've met with no unpleasantness," he said. "No jibes at all?"

"None that I can recall, sir, I assure you."

"Surely we're not that gutless," Larry said. "If we are, if we're really as accepting as you say, then we deserve to be overrun."

"You'd rather not have our American friends here?" Ruth looked directly at Larry.

"That's right. It's too complicated, and it's dangerous."

"It's unnecessary also," Douglas added. "Though of course there's a difference between you as a human being, Robert, and you as a representative of a nation with a particular political position."

"Thank you, sir, and that's just what I've been alluding to. You Scots do us the courtesy of looking behind the uniform and welcoming us as human beings."

"What I'd like to know," Larry asked, "is whether you too look behind the uniform, see yourself as a human being who happens to be a navy man or just as a navy man?"

Smiling, crew-cut, Robert scanned the ceiling before replying.

"I'm a navy man first, I'd say. That's how I think of myself anyway. I've signed on for a long term and I don't think I'd have done that if I didn't find great meaning in the job."

Ruth turned to him.

"I've not heard you say that sort of thing before."

"You've not asked me." Robert was smiling brightly. "For all you care, I might be a fireman or a policeman."

"That's not fair and you know it!"

"You mean," Larry interrupted, "that the fact that he's a naval officer is part of his attraction?"

"Do I really have to answer that?"

"Why not?" Larry pressed.

"All I can say," she responded pertly, putting on an American accent, "is that I don't think I can trust a man who can't distinguish himself from his job."

A silence fell. Ruth looked slightly hurt, Larry vaguely expectant, and Robert was still smiling. They all then looked to Douglas.

"And who are you, Ruth?" he asked.

She clasped the knee of her right leg, rocking slightly before replying, "That's some question!"

"Maybe, but isn't it preferable to the usual one – what do you do?"

"I suppose so."

His mood of calm was going, Douglas knew. He hoped he would be able to turn the conversation in a more agreeable direction. Then he would go to bed. What happened after that was not his responsibility. He realised he didn't find either of the visitors particularly engaging. He wondered what Larry saw in them. If the occasion arose, he would ask him, he would offer his impressions and compare them with his son's. It might be a way of helping him to be more discriminating. Again it struck him that idle curiosity was one of Larry's worst vices. Essential to purge him of it. Essential.

"It's six hours on and six hours off when we're at sea," Robert said suddenly, "right through the twenty-four hours, day after day, weekends not excepted. You've got to be very adaptable, to be able to go with little sleep. Some find it very hard."

"And who asked you?" Ruth said. "It was I who was about to account for myself."

"On you go then."

"Full steam ahead," Larry said.

"Actually I don't do anything," Ruth said in an irritated voice. "I'm rather like Yvonne, I suppose, only I'm not loaded. In October I'm going to St Andrews University to study English and Politics, but until then I'm staying at home."

"Home is with your parents?" Douglas asked.

"Yes," she said briskly, as if some criticism might have been intended. "Daddy's chairman of Fairfax and Jackson."

Douglas had seen vans and lorries from Fairfax and Jackson in the neighbourhood. They were bright blue, with the name, Fairfax and Jackson, in bright red. As far as he could remember, they were naval architects or naval engineers – something like that. The vans and lorries always looked very new, as though out on their first trip that day. Once, hurrying home to Edith, he had gone into a ditch to avoid one. The driver had been very courteous, winding down his window to ask if Douglas was all right, then jumping down to help, his uniform bright blue like the van, the name, Fairfax and Jackson, bright red on his lapels.

"I see," Douglas said, wondering why the fact that Ruth's

father was the chairman of Fairfax and Jackson had emptied him of all desire to question her further. Was it the fact itself, or how she had presented it, girlishly offhand, or something else?

"Would you like to see father's observatory, Ruth?" Larry asked. "You mentioned you had an interest in the stars."

"I believe they have a great influence on us," she said.

"I'm an astronomer," Douglas responded, "not an astrologer."

"Even so, I'd really appreciate it if you could …"

"You must excuse me, I'm afraid. I've just come down from three hours up there. Anyway, there's not that much to see."

"Robert?" Larry asked.

"No thanks. But don't let me stop the two of you."

Ruth was on her feet, suddenly eager.

"I suppose, if you're interested in the ocean depths, you're unlikely to be interested in the stars also," she said.

Robert said nothing.

A wind had got up. When Larry and Ruth went outside, there was a rush of air in the hall. The coat stand was blown against the wall, papers and magazines on a low table agitated, pictures shaken where they hung. Then, the front door closing, it was still again.

As far as Douglas knew, Larry had never looked through a telescope seriously. He had allowed him to take it up with him because otherwise the trip would have been pointless. First he would have to set it up, then focus it, then find a part of the heavens to concentrate on. He pictured him, awkwardly gallant, inviting Ruth to have the first look, standing behind her in the darkness of the hut, not knowing what to say either about the stars or the occasion. He suspected that unless something interested her immediately, Ruth would turn away, complaining of the cold, the night, the vastnesses of space. They would be back quickly, quarter of an hour or so, entering the cottage in another burst of wind maybe, lights swaying, curtains billowing, pictures shaken. Meanwhile he would have to make what he could of the imperturbable submariner. Then bed.

"It's not as if I don't have my responsibilities and attachments," Robert began suddenly, as if he had been waiting to be alone with Douglas, older man and confidant, all evening. "I do, I certainly do. There are my parents and my three sisters, fine people all of them. My father has an engineering business and one of my sisters works with him there. My other two sisters are married, both pregnant actually. My father had hopes I might become an engineer too, but no one supported me more when I decided to join the navy."

Again Douglas had the sense of a prepared speech. Perhaps any older man would have been subjected to it.

"And I have a girl. Her name is Angie. A childhood sweetheart."

"Have you told her about Ruth, or Ruth about her?" Douglas was conscious of a wish to unsettle Robert.

"Well, sir, that's an astute question, but since I've not compromised myself with Ruthie, I've not felt an obligation to tell either about the other."

"Either about the other …"

"Beg pardon?"

"Either about the other: it just sounds strange."

"Yes, I suppose it does."

"But if you were to compromise yourself, as you put it, with Ruth …"

"Then certainly I'd come clean. Oh certainly."

"More men have two women than you might think."

"I'll have to take your word for that, sir."

Looking at Robert's unusually bright eyes and noting how they always seemed to be taken up with something just behind you, Douglas wondered if he might be on drugs. His impeccable manners and scrupulous kind of conversation then seemed possible further symptoms, overcompensations for a tendency to drift into vagueness. He had heard

70

that drugs were a problem on submarines, the real social cement, officers and ratings at one in their dependence, none of it admitted though. He tried to catch Robert's eye and hold it, but failed. What he thought was that the eyes were brighter than one would expect in such a face. They glistened or glittered, as in anticipation of some saving disclosure, nervous in case it should not happen, desperate for it. Nothing in the present seemed truly honoured.

"I write to Angie every week and she writes to me. I have some hopes that she'll be able to come over later this year. I'd like to take her on a tour of the highlands. I hear the landscape is historic up there."

"Pre-historic …"

"Yes."

"They're certainly worth a visit. Several visits."

"Perhaps, before we go, you'd be willing to suggest an itinerary or two?"

"I'd be glad to."

In the silence which followed Douglas became relaxed again. He didn't want to talk or listen any more. He breathed evenly, felt his pulse slow, felt Robert recede. Was this how it was for Edith in meditation?

Then Larry and Ruth returned; they had been away for about forty minutes. There was a quietness between them which Douglas was willing to see as contentment rather than disaffection. Even to the ignorant eye, he knew, the heavens could be calming.

Later, he woke to hear Larry bidding his guests goodbye, but he couldn't tell from the tone or pitch of his voice how the evening had ended.

Edith's Journal – 3

Larry has been mixing with Americans. Because of this girl, Ruth. Douglas told me about her. Perhaps he fancies her himself, he was so vague. He couldn't give me a clear picture. As if – if he did – I'd be jealous – her youth, looks, figure etc. But really, I'm beyond all that; not a competitor any more. What he did say was that Larry was making a play for her, not an entirely unsuccessful one, either. I'd be so glad to have him know some happiness. It would push back the failures a bit, the pain …

Anyway, because he's been meeting Americans, we know that they're nervous about the marches. That surprised me. I'd have thought that by now marches would have held no terrors for them. After so many years. I remember the early ones. I could walk then. I really thought that something would come of it; it wouldn't have surprised me to hear that the establishment feared us. But it's different now. There's no passion in it: people march piously, automatically, and that's useless, isn't it?

I couldn't stand to be pushed on a march, not even by Douglas and Larry. You'd think there must be another way. What with all this pain, I could become a bomb: I sometimes think it. But pain is useless; so far as I can see, it serves no purposes at all. On the contrary, it muddies me at the centre and at the edges. Better not read this over in case I score it out. Dip the pen in my pain and keep on. What else?

What happens in crowds is that I lose all sense of the person pushing me. It doesn't happen otherwise; I always know it's Larry or Douglas there. It would be like this on a march: it could be anyone pushing me. What's worse, I could be anyone being pushed! By the end of the march I'd not care about anything because the me who does the caring wouldn't be there to care. A body pushing a body – that's all. Anything more pointless I can't imagine. One should engage in protests with all one's wits about one. Hot with enlightened rage. I couldn't even rely on my pain to sustain me because, being part of me, it goes when I go. (Sometimes I think we stand or fall together, my pain and I.) Other wheelchair cases say similar things, unless they're very stupid. Too long pushed in a crowd and you become nothing. One I spoke to even contrived to fall from his chair under such circumstances: it was like pulling the communication cord, he said.

All said and done, therefore, I'll not be on the Easter march. I'll either do nothing or something out of the ordinary. But what can cripples do that is out of the ordinary? I could try meditation, I suppose, but that's the least public of acts, and there are times when something very public is called for. I could start screaming, as I was told another cripple once did in a railway station. She'd never done it before, and never did it again (her husband saw to that). But it was effective; the train waited for her for twenty minutes. But nobody would know what I was screaming at. Nobody would give me credit for using my old lungs for political purposes. I'd be dismissed as crazy, distracted by pain, brain damaged.

So whatever I do, it must be clear why I'm doing it. Its significance must be plain. I'll turn to the past, I think, busy myself with protests through the ages. A comforting thought. An inspiring one, actually. Redeemed by earlier times. I often think, you see, that we've become becalmed in this crazy present of ours, that we can only be liberated by the past. It's as if the hands of various ages are constantly held out to us ... How true what they say: it takes a crisis for you to know your friends, even if they're all dead. Winstanley, Bunyan, Danton ...

I think that whatever I do, it must be a surprise, especially to my family. Oh certainly it must be a surprise. Otherwise they may try to talk me out of it, and that would be bad, for I'll need all my energy. Anyway, they do say, don't they, that true protest is solitary, hatched in the darkness but then shedding light?

VI

One day in late February Helen sent word that Barnie had died in his sleep. "While resting" was her actual phrase. She would contact Douglas after the funeral, she said.

This meant, Douglas knew, that after a decent interval she would begin to look for a cottage along the coast. It was her plan. It meant, too, that the next stage, Edith's death and Helen's coming to live with him had moved closer. The thought neither heartened nor disheartened him. It was a happening too closely shadowed by the deaths of their partners to be clearly imagined, if imagined at all. He had no particular feelings about it, which at times was embarrassing. How judge if you should do something if you felt little? He tried to tell himself that it would happen if it was meant to happen, but because he didn't really know what this meant, it didn't help.

She moved more quickly than he had thought, just a week after the funeral phoning to ask if he would take her to see a cottage.

He met her from the ferry, collected the cottage keys from the estate agent, and, feeling strange with her, out of touch, set off along the coast road. It was raining, and the sound of the windscreen wipers, loud and insistent, framed their silences. It struck Douglas that, if death played games, one of them was to come between lovers, subvert ease and understanding. When they spoke, their remarks seemed pointless, their enquiries forced and insincere, and, when they fell silent again, it was like another failure.

They had discussed, of course, how they imagined they would be affected by these deaths, how, in spite of their patience, their striving for humility, it might seem as if they had willed them. This was now quite close, Douglas thought, to how he felt: as if he didn't own himself, didn't deserve to either. His body felt slack, boneless almost, and he drove badly, stalling, miscalculating on the bends, speeding up and slowing down like a learner.

Once, feeling how bad it must be for Helen, and as if to assure her that the awkwardness would pass, he put out a hand, but she didn't respond.

Then he saw that she was crying. He passed her some tissues, but she made no move to take them. As if it was the very least that she could do, she let the tears course unattended down her cheeks. He thought it was the most silent weeping he had known. Like that of a ghost. Body mortified, tears free. He spoke her name twice, but as though into a medium which killed both voice and name.

Eventually he pulled off the road, hoping that in the silence and with the loch before them they would find a way of coming together. They didn't. He wished he hadn't stopped; it had been easier in the moving car. He couldn't move off so soon though without making an effort, without – as by some act of will – trying to summon up his love for her.

Only the sound of rain now. Quickly the car became steamed up. Douglas wiped the windscreen with a rag. It seemed important at least to be able to see the loch. But within minutes it had steamed up again. He tried once more to take her hand, but all he could feel were knuckles. Her profile too had a compacted look, as if her spirit was turning in on itself.

He surprised himself then, getting decisively out of the car and wiping the windscreen from the outside. Dimly inside he could see Helen, hunched, leaning to one side, staring straight ahead of her. Seeing her through the rain and the windscreen was like seeing her under water, he thought, victim of some kind of accident, adrift in another element.

He walked down the road a little. It was raining very heavily. There was a mist over the loch, silver as aluminium foil. It was not thick enough though to conceal the black shapes of submarines moving seawards. So strongly did they compel his attention that, as if it was what they had come for, the object of all their searches, he pointed at them and exclaimed loudly. They were very black and vertical, bows sharp and easy, conning towers streaming with rain.

Fearing breathlessness, he expanded his chest, took some deep breaths with his eyes shut. In the time it took him to do so, the submarines vanished, whether into the mist or the loch itself he didn't know. Only for an instant did he think he had imagined them. Gulls cried, very close by, but he couldn't see them.

Approaching the car, he saw nothing. What was she doing behind the steamed up windows? How persuade her to come out? He didn't want to get back in; it would trouble his breathing, he was sure, the confined space, the steamed up windows, the silences.

He wondered if this was why the adulterer died before his faithful neighbour? The burden of two lives. The necessity of them too though. God yes.

He worked at his breathing again, head back, chest out. Then, with the energy this seemed to give him ("Breathe and live," the consultant had said, "breathe and live"), he roughly opened the door.

Helen appeared to be asleep, curled up, leaning against the door. He stood over her in silence for a moment. She didn't move. Some sort of simulation of death or dying or sleep? A hysterical precision to it which exasperated him. He hadn't seen it in her before. Hoped never to see it in her again.

He leant solicitously forwards, as he supposed she wanted him to, anticipating both further unresponsiveness and the exasperation this would cause him. Then – touching her shoulder – experiencing these exactly.

"Come out!" he said. "Come out! We can walk here. At least that. Stop this!"

Once again she didn't respond, so he grabbed her by the wrist and pulled. She didn't resist, but didn't submit either. Eventually he got her into a crouching position, half way out of the car, the skills he had developed over the years with Edith having come in handy. She was starting to laugh, as if it was a game gone wrong.

"Edith can't actually manage this sort of thing at all, you know!"

"Do I really want to come and live here?" Bitterly abstracted, she shook herself free of him. "Do I?"

"I don't know. Do you? We've discussed it often enough. It seemed a good idea once."

"Submarines below and jets above." She spoke theatrically, pirouetting a little. "It'd set my teeth on edge."

"My teeth aren't on edge and I live here. There's more to the place than jets and submarines."

"It's an end-of-the-world sort of place."

"Well described," Douglas said, nodding. "It's what I've said before. You can't become complacent here; it's too representative …"

"I wonder if I quite know what you mean after all." Interrupting him, she turned away.

"You can't buy butter without being aware of the world's worst drift. It's bracing, to say the least."

"But in retirement? Do we really need such reminders in retirement? Don't we already know?"

"We do, but we're good at forgetting. Anyway, when better than in retirement? We've time to think, come to a reckoning."

They stared out across the loch in silence. The rain had lightened, become drizzle.

"I can get you to the midday ferry," Douglas said presently.

He had known for some moments that he was going to

say this. What he hadn't known was that, having said it, he was going to wipe the rain very gently from her face and hair. Her tight white curls were beginning to soften, stick to her skull, and her eyes, if not mild, had a kind of fading strictness.

"I ought at least to see the cottage first."

"I'll take you."

"What were you pointing at earlier?"

"Oh, did you see me? Submarines. I was pointing at submarines. They were out there, in and out of the mist like phantoms. They're on endless exercises, I've come to realise. A kind of endless flexing. Same with the jets. Our lives here are certainly stretched out on the network of these. But not to breaking point. They aren't the bottom line."

"What is then?"

"Silence, I think."

"Oh? And what's that supposed to mean?"

"Silence: it stands for peace and all that peace makes possible. In silence we can work at peace, we can think, meditate ..."

"Like Edith?"

"Like Edith, yes. War is the interruption of peace, you see, not peace of war."

"I suppose, at our age, such simplicities are forgivable."

"Is that all they are?"

"The way I'm feeling today, all this guilty sadness, this dire," she waved her hand, seeking the word with difficulty, "regret, that is how they seem, yes."

"You'll be coming on the march though?" The quiet way he asked it, it seemed like another simplicity.

"I suppose so." She smiled. "If you're going."

Her manner made him feel unadventurous, fainthearted. A man for petitions, letters to the newspapers, marches. Worthy democratic ways.

He opened the car door for her, but she didn't immediately get in. Something about the scene seemed to be holding her; it was as if she was trying to memorise it. Sensing the depths, of anger and disaffection and dread, from which she was doing so, Douglas realised that he envied her. Such depths! Once he had feared them, their effect on his health, but not now. Now it was their denial he thought might do damage. Ambiguous nourishment. To follow your nose and let your breathing take care of itself. To court extremes, enjoy the shaping energy they brought.

"You see, I can't believe we've chosen to retire here just to be spectators," Helen said. "We may not know what we're here for, but we can try to find out."

"A destiny behind the obvious one, d'you mean?"

"Something like that. Isn't that what's supposed to happen in old age – an unexpected flowering?"

"It's what I was trying to get at earlier, I think. To retire here is to be challenged. A flowering becomes more likely."

"We're in agreement then. Who'd have known it? I'm sorry." She spoke gravely, close to tears. "It's taken us so long to get here, hasn't it, and I don't just mean here the agreement, but here the place."

During this last exchange, they had wandered a little way from the car. Now, arm in arm, they returned to it.

The cottage was about seventy yards from the coast road, a low white building with small windows and thick walls. A line of beech trees protected it from the road and marked the start of a garden. Behind was a grassy cliff which Douglas thought might once have been a quarry. Bushes and little trees grew from it sideways, straining for the vertical.

Because of the mist, there wasn't much of a view, but Douglas said that on a good day he was sure it would be excellent. They couldn't hear much either; the cliff had a way of deadening sound. When they called out "Hullo", the echoes died almost immediately.

For a moment or two, as if wondering whether to enter, they considered the house from close up.

"At least you'll not be able to see the base from here," Douglas said. "It's round the headland."

"I wouldn't mind if I did. I've never gone much for the picturesque."

Except for a white telephone on a directory in the middle of the lounge, the cottage was entirely empty. It was hard to believe, such was the smell of dampness, that it had only recently been vacated. With no curtains or carpets to soften or subdue, their voices and footsteps seemed too loud for the rooms, which were small anyway and gloomy. They also appeared to Douglas to slope downwards from the door, undulating slightly as they did so. Beneath the floorboards there was an impression of hard rock, some granite substratum; above, there were wooden beams, smoke darkened.

Always behind Helen in his inspections, Douglas sometimes found himself walking on tiptoe.

He didn't want to influence her either way. He knew though that unless they chose to live apart, not risk it together, it would be a choice one day between his cottage and this one. He could tell from the way she lingered at each doorway, each window, that she was having similar thoughts and struggling to keep them to herself. Death the inadmissible pawn on the board of their hopes and desires. Almost silently therefore they went from room to room, Helen's main response being to sniff the dampness now and then, and seem to be about to speak.

"It'll do," Helen said at last. "I'm not as fussy as I used to be. Yes! Why bother to look any further? Save my energy. I'll have to sell a lot, though; this'll only take about a third of what I have."

Douglas couldn't imagine the place furnished and welcoming in any season. His voice boomed in the bare room.

"A little work and it'll be fine. And if you don't like it …"

"Don't worry, I fully intend to make a go of it." She didn't sound bitter exactly but nor did she seem entirely reconciled. "There's no alternative."

She had her back to him, rubbing her left calf with her right foot. Her light brown waistcoat was tightly belted, her hands deep in its pockets. He moved towards her, but seeing her suddenly in profile – a kind of self-consuming strictness – stopped, turned away. A second silence seemed to descend on the first, the bareness of the room to spread. He felt that all he could do was touch her, whether he wanted to or not.

There had been a time when he wouldn't have done it, wouldn't have touched her unless he had desired her; but he knew better now, he thought. The polite touch better than none at all. The unexpected spiritedness of flesh.

He felt too that something ought to be done to mark her decision to buy the place. It was brave of her, he thought. About to touch her, however, he didn't recognise himself. Didn't recognise her either. Only her body was familiar, and even it had a kind of penumbra of pain and strangeness. Closing his eyes, he put his arms round her and held her from behind.

After a while he slipped his right hand under her coat and began to caress her breasts. She shifted in his arms, but he couldn't tell if it was desire or unease. Nothing was said. No sounds at all. He continued to caress her.

Then, suddenly, he bowed his head, as in apology almost, and kissed her on the neck. She lifted her head a little. Out of confused bereavement, a sign, however uncertain. She didn't want him, but wanted to want him. Perhaps that.

His desire was strong now, but he knew it mustn't be apparent. He could only bring her round if he appeared as troubled as she. She would respond to his confusion, not to his desire. He kissed her again on the neck, feeling that it was not just the next few hours that were at stake, but the next few weeks and even months as well. Worse, that if he didn't arouse her now – in this bare cottage gradually filling with mist – he mightn't be able to do so again. He continued to hold her from behind therefore, moaning a little, his passion pitched painfully between faith and despair, groundless for the time, blind.

At last, boldly, she turned to him, giving him a quick look, then kissing him full on the mouth. He kissed her back, gripping her buttocks, lowering himself to her a little. Outside, he thought he heard something, a twig snapping, a bird passing, some trick of the wind. Inside, the silence excited him – an inviting barrenness. A fog-horn sounded. Too many promontories, he thought. A dangerous coast. The mist would have wound its way up from it, from the loch, but would have come first from the sea, bred there. It was definitely a presence in the cottage as they kissed. He had a sense of it as come from all quarters to be with them, participate with them in whatever they were about to venture. He thought he heard the sound again, again was able to dismiss it: just one of many small sounds that prey on country silence.

Abruptly Helen broke away, saying they should lay their overcoats on the floor. She was flexing her fingers, pointing at a particular spot on the floor with her right toe.

"It'll have to be quick, and you'll have to take me. Come on!"

"D'you not …"

"Hurry!"

"I don't …"

"I'm beneath it for the time being. Beneath everything in fact." She spoke desperately. "Hurry!"

Suddenly, then, she was dancing backwards, pirouetting. And when she wasn't, she was lifting her skirt, jigging. Douglas was both aroused and appalled. He believed he knew what it meant though. It wasn't that she was bereaved as terribly ashamed that she wasn't. Or wasn't more so. He went after her, caught up with her in a corner, almost violent now, his desire become a desire to release her from this latest darkness.

He forced her onto the raincoats.

"I do believe I'm hysterical." She was tossing her head from side to side. "I do believe that!"

"Don't say anything. It'll be alright."

Legs raised, she began to laugh and it seemed to Douglas as he prepared to enter her like a parody of all the laughter he had ever heard. "My love," he murmured.

"No!" she cried. "No!"

Now however it was not just the mist that was about them, circulating in the cottage as if it too had its purposes. As in its wake came the most dreadful smell, a smell as of drains, sewers. It came in waves, each worse than the one before, so that it was impossible not to imagine that the cause of it wasn't advancing towards them also – some tide of silage or sewage or decomposing bodies even over fields and woodland, through hedges, ditches.

Helen had stood up.

"What a smell!" She was looking at the door.

"What is it?"

"I don't know. I've never smelt anything like it."

"Nor I."

"It seems to be rising from the earth."

"Miasma."

"What?"

"Miasma."

"Yes."

Next the sky was full of noise, a roar from all quarters, jets above them, wave upon wave of them, flying very low. Standing at the front door, they could see them very clearly. First they went under the mist, then into it, then out of it again, up and over the wooded hills on the other side of the loch. It took about five minutes for them to pass, and even after they had gone, vanished into the west somewhere, the sky was still loud with them, the earth trembling.

Hand in hand, they had forgotten about the smell, but now in the returning silence became aware of it again, as bad as before, as engulfing.

Round the side of the cottage, then, Douglas heard the sound again. A kind of scuffling at first, then chuckling, low and surreptitious. Had they been seen? He imagined someone bent double with mirth at the sight of a man in late middle age about to enter a woman also in late middle age. There was a short silence, and, when the sound came again, it was not chuckling they heard but cackling. Out of laboured breathing it struggled to a kind of crescendo, sank briefly into the breathing again before starting upwards once more. There seemed no limit to it, each climax of mirth more intense than the one before.

Indicating that Helen should stay where she was, Douglas moved to the side of the cottage. Not any kind of courage but simple curiosity drove him. Who was it? Was there any connection between the intruder and the smell? He didn't think there could be, but the thought persisted, perhaps because the smell was so bad now, truly rising as though from the earth. Rounding the corner, he had his hand to his mouth.

It was an old woman, toothless and so enormously fat it gave her coat, riding up over her backside and stomach, the look of a waistcoat.

She was grinning and licking her lips and making a humming noise. She was also holding out her hands, as if it was Douglas, not herself, who was the intruder. Her face and hands were rough and ruddy, as though made so somehow by her bulk, and there was no break between her jaw and thick, goitred throat. Douglas expected a strong voice, a definite accent, rustic perhaps. But when she spoke it was with genteel precision. At first he took it to be parody, some kind of parody of the middle classes, and thought that at any moment her real voice would come through. Through exaggeratedly pursed lips however came quaint phrases, genteel inflections. Her handshake was genteel too, a mere hint or caress.

Then she was walking beside the cottage wall, hugging it. Douglas stepped aside to let her pass. From behind she looked even worse, buttocks huge and the seam of her coat split from the shoulders downwards. She was cackling again.

By the time she reached Helen, however, she was talking very rapidly. Newly risen from hysteria, Helen looked distressed and astonished behind the spate of words. It was like glimpsing someone through water. Douglas winked at her, raised his eyebrows.

"Yes, oh yes, I once lived here with my late husband, Arthur. We were so very happy! When he died, I lived on alone. Each day I expected him to return. It wasn't right without him. Actually it felt very wrong. Still does. When I absolutely knew that he wasn't coming back, I sold the cottage to a young couple called the Stevensons. They were childless and unhealthy and split up after two years. Children might have saved them; I told them so in a letter, but they didn't reply. Once later on I met Diane Stevenson in town. She was crying, couldn't stop. I took her in for a coffee but she was crying so much she couldn't swallow it. Then there were the Farquharsons, an older couple who kept to themselves and stayed for seven years. He – Macgregor Farquharson – sometimes on summer evenings played the horn, or was it the trombone, in the garden. Just there. He'd stand up to do it. I can hear it still … When he died, his wife Alice sold up and moved to a small flat in Glasgow but died there almost immediately. She'd have been better to stay put, if you ask me. Moving kills. There would have been good ghosts to sustain her, Arthur and I, farming people from the last century … Her daughter rented it out for a while to a naval couple called the Wotherspoons, Ted and Rhonda, but they hated the navy and soon moved to Dorset to start a zoo or was it a bed and breakfast, I can't remember. It's been empty since then. I'd buy it back if I was younger, but I'm nearly eighty and Arthur won't be coming back now. Are you thinking of buying? I do hope so. It's a happy place, in spite of all. With its own bird life too! There was a heron used to surprise us, sweeping down from the escarpment of a summer evening. First there would be its shadow, then it – whoosh! Owls too, you will find, are wedded to the place, as are martins."

"Would you happen to know what the smell is?" Helen asked. "It's perfectly awful."

"In our day everything smelled very natural, as though just created. But these new fertilisers are bad, not to mention all the rubbish that gathers on the shore and that definitely smells in hot weather. Then there's the nuclear stuff, the danger of leaks and all that. We had some destroyers and cruisers at rest on the loch in the years after the war, very grey, like ghosts they were, but that was all. It was very beautiful then and given a chance could be again. But will it be? Who knows? Oh the rooms will be lovely when you furnish them, I assure you. Now they're just caves. I'd recommend thick carpets by the way, and thick curtains. The escarpment has a cold breath – we always said that. I should just say that I have a name – Fiona Agnes Flood. How do you do! I'm not really alone, for I have a daughter in Tasmania and two cats. The cats and I live in town. We can see the cottage from the top room. Oh I do hope you'll put in an offer. I'd say you were made for the place."

She turned then and went into the cottage. They could hear her going from room to room, muttering to herself, cackling. Helen gripped Douglas' hand. When she came back, she seemed bigger than ever, almost too big for the front door, her breath white on the whiteness of the mist, her mouth making a sucking sound.

"Goodbye then." As if she regretted now having gone on at such length, she spoke quietly. "God bless."

She moved quickly for a woman of her age and bulk, once or twice, as though impelled by her weight, venturing a little trot. Soon she had gained the road and her car. Its headlights pierced the mist. Then she was gone.

By the time they set off for the afternoon ferry, the mist had lifted. Pale sunlight fell on the still waters of the loch, making them look oily.

At once poignant and grotesque, the episode with Fiona Flood had shaken them out of themselves. They laughed at it, laughed at her overcoat and her accent and her cackling and her turns of phrase. They even laughed at the terrible smell, the way in which, as though a product of old age and obesity, it had seemed to leak from her pores.

Douglas took a road he hadn't noticed before. Wooded on one side, steep and rocky on the other, it ran for about five miles. At regular intervals on the steep side there were dark slits in the hillside, silos, Douglas knew, waiting missiles. An ancient hillside put to new uses. He could see trenches, wire, embankments. Rather like the anti-aircraft posts of the Second World War, he thought, some of which still survived.

They didn't speak, feeling as though they were being watched. One or two patches of mist clung to the higher slopes. Douglas looked closely, to see if they weren't perhaps sheep. No sheep here, of course. None at all. As if some dream of pastoral ease was mocking him, though, he continued to see them as such, the silos as sheep pens. The absurdity of it made him laugh. Worse than absurdity. Helen laughed too, more wildly than he. She had a hand on his arm as, going very slowly now, peering from side to side, they came to the end of the glen, began to emerge from it, its calamitous stillness.

When it left the glen, the road went sharply downhill, through hairpin bends, to the shore. The mere fact of descending, of falling away from something towards sea-level, brought relief. The loch was flat calm, colourless, without traffic. To their right, hundreds of seagulls rose suddenly from a ploughed field and flew away raggedly before them. Soon they had settled on the loch, briefly as motionless there as the water itself, but before Douglas and Helen arrived they were off again, some going for the far shore, some for the open sea. For a few moments their cries – casual, violent, beguiling – were all that could be heard, and, when they ceased, Douglas thought that he could hear the echoes, now before him, now behind him, tearing at the silence.

"I'll make a bid for it," Helen said suddenly. "In spite of the smell."

"I would, if I were you. Anyway, smells can be treated."

"Yes."

At first they had the road to themselves, but after about two miles they came on a queue of cars. There were flashing lights at the front – blue, orange – and men in uniform, police and American navy personnel. Douglas turned off the engine; they were in good time for the ferry and could sit quietly. The flashing lights made it difficult however. Then they heard shouting, sounds rather than words, but after a while words as well – "no business!" "Yanks!" "no favours!" They were the voices of young men. Douglas became uneasy – something to do with the pitch of the voices, some quality of stubbornness and intemperance they had, seemed to be exulting in. Helen, who had been looking out of the window, reported that two young men were being marched towards them.

Marching and shouting, Douglas mused – you rarely heard them together. It was one or the other. Now, for instance, when the marching stopped, you would probably hear the shouting again. Exactly so. The marching did stop, abruptly, decisively, as though commanded to, and instantly the shouting came again, louder than before, wordless and raucous and with its own impetus, putting Douglas in mind of underground streams, muddied and impure, gathering further impurities as they went, surfacing now here, now there.

If the voices were familiar, it was, Douglas believed, because he had heard such voices raised in anger over so many years. In the schools he had taught in; in the streets; on television; in the dead of night. They all sounded the same and wearied him now.

What he saw at first were two figures stumbling in silhouette against the pale, gently shimmering loch. In another age they might have been flagellants, he thought, but in this they were two of the insulted and injured.

Then he saw that one of them was Larry. He and his companion, arms twisted behind their backs, were being pushed along the grass verge by two policemen. Military police followed.

"It's my son," Douglas said. "It's Larry."

Larry looked as if he had been in a fight. His clothes and face were dusty, his hair was sticking out in tufts from his head, and he was breathing heavily. His recognition of his father was so long delayed that Douglas wondered if he was trying to ignore him. But, when it came, the recognition was immediate and profound. Taking Douglas' hand, holding onto it, he explained to his companion (how typical that Douglas didn't know him) and the policemen that this was his father. He said it strangely, with a kind of dry emphasis. A crowd of about a dozen heard him and seemed to approve.

"Is this true sir?" one of the policemen asked.

"Yes, it is."

Father and son were still holding hands. They made a little joke of it now, lifting their hands in mock triumph to the crowd.

"Then I have to inform you that we're arresting your son and his companion for disturbing the peace."

"It was a peaceful protest," the companion said in a loud voice.

"Larry?" Douglas asked.

"Certainly it was peaceful, until two Americans butted in, that is."

"That's right," one of the policemen said.

"Then why haven't the Americans been arrested too?" Larry asked.

"Because in our opinion it was you who started it."

"If you can believe that, you can believe anything," the companion said.

"I must ask you to come along to the station now. You can come too, sir, if you want."

"Certainly I will. There seems to be some confusion."

"Oh I wouldn't say that, sir," the policeman said.

Dusk was beginning to fall and mist to rise again from the loch and fields as they followed the police car into town. Larry and his companion sat in the back, squashed between the two policemen. Douglas drove with his eyes glued to the back of his son's head. He was looking to see if even in the back of a police car and under arrest the head would roll about. It did. Probably he was trying to make light of the occasion. He would be cracking bad jokes. The other heads were completely still. He pointed the phenomenon out to Helen, adding that the head had been rolling about like this since birth. He had never seen such a head.

"Heavy with brains," Helen said.

"More brains than judgement."

"Oh?"

"Whether it's women or politics, he miscalculates."

"He's not miscalculated just because he's been caught."

"I know."

"At least he's done something." She seemed to give in to some private vexation. "You must see that."

"He had a girlfriend recently, I think," Douglas said, speaking very slowly, as if for the moment he couldn't be sure of anything, "but he didn't keep her. He never does."

"Too eager?"

"Eagerness can be attractive, but not in him."

"What d'you mean exactly?"

"In him it becomes something else, a kind of monomania, I fear, everyone to dance to his tune. Except that he's not really got a tune."

He was surprised to hear himself talking about Larry like this. He didn't know what he was trying to do: apologise for his awkward son in advance, or brace himself for the possibility that the "peaceful protest" had been quite ridiculously botched. Both perhaps. If Helen imagined there were elevated motives, she would be disappointed, almost certainly. On the public stage Larry would probably always be a ludicrous figure, idly curious, mimicking gravity. "Public stage" wasn't even an appropriate image, for Larry would never choose to go on it. He would be dragged, following a ruse which had gone wrong, he would be tripped.

The police car drew up at a long low building in a street near to the ferry terminal. Larry got out and made as if to go over to his father. But was called back. Certain things weren't permitted now apparently. He was told to stand by his companion. With his foot then he traced something in the dirt by the pavement and smirked. His companion ignored him. He traced something else, again was ignored. Douglas wondered how long they had been acquainted. He wouldn't have been surprised to discover that they had met only that day, in a pub at lunch-time perhaps, to be arrested together some hours later for abusing American servicemen. Or for staging a protest. What sort of protest though and in what sort of spirit staged? The answers to these questions might never be found, he realised. Larry might never be able to come clean.

"I can see you don't take your son's actions very

seriously," Helen said. "You know him as well as anyone, of course, but … may he not have come of age today?"

"I don't think I follow you," Douglas said, although he suspected he probably did. "Come of age?"

"By making a protest. Simply that. By objecting to the American presence here." She was looking at him very directly, her colour high, her eyes moist.

"That's possible, I suppose, but it's more likely to have been a drunken whim."

"I can imagine something starting as a drunken whim becoming serious. Can't you?"

"Come and meet him anyway," Douglas said, thinking that in some respects Larry and Helen had more in common than either had with him.

He hadn't imagined that they would meet for some time. But now they shook hands as if they had been hearing good reports of each other for years. Larry then introduced them to his companion, David, a young man with glittering eyes and an uneasy manner who looked from Douglas to Helen and back again.

"All we did was tell them they had no business blocking the road for so long," David said. "You know those long articulated lorries they drive with those missiles nobody in their right mind wants? One of them. We were polite."

"That's right," Larry said, "but if your opinions aren't acceptable, you're in trouble if you express them."

"It's not a free country," David said.

"It never was," Helen added.

Meeting Larry and David had excited Helen. Douglas couldn't remember seeing her like it before. Under the bright lights of the police station he could see that she was flushed, a flush which had spread right up to her scalp where, under her thin white curls, it suggested a birthmark. Hugging her handbag, moving from foot to foot, she seemed to be trying to ingratiate herself. Douglas felt uncomfortable. The radicalism of middle age trying to befriend that of youth. One of the phoney alliances, he feared.

He stepped back and away from them, wondering why they were still standing outside the station. He asked one of the policemen who replied pointedly that since there had been several such incidents in the course of the day, the station was full. They would have to wait their turn.

Out of her excitement, Helen suddenly announced that she would have to go. Her ferry was approaching, she could see its lights from where she stood. She shook Larry and David by the hand, wished them luck and said that she hoped very much to meet them again. Then, kissing Douglas lightly on the mouth, she ran, neatly and self-consciously, still hugging her handbag, towards the ferry terminal, once stopping to wave, the wave as excited as her departure, a kind of irreverent flourish in the gathering dusk.

"Nice woman," Larry said. "Who is she?"

"Later," Douglas said. "Let's get this sorted out first."

When they came out of the police station, Larry and David charged with disturbing the peace on a public high-way and resisting arrest, it was dark and raining heavily. David asked to be dropped off at a housing estate on the outskirts of the town. He said he would give Larry a ring in a few days: they could have a drink, talk things over.

Almost as if they had achieved something long desired and planned, so that there was now nothing to say, Douglas and Larry drove on in silence.

"I suspect your mother has been in a lot of pain recently," Douglas said after a bit. "I don't think this evening would be the best time to tell her about this afternoon. I think we should wait."

"Have you ever considered," Larry suddenly burst out, "that it's never quite knowing, not being properly told, always being so considerately kept in the dark, that's made her ill? Or, if not exactly that, that's keeping her ill and may be making her worse? She can't move, in that sense can't act, so the very least we can do is keep her informed, tell her what we're up to, down to the last detail let her share in our efforts, our daring, if daring it is. She believes that we who can walk don't do enough with our mobility. Did you know that? Did you know that she thinks that? She can only go into the world, go at the world, through us, so we must be a lot more active than we are and we must keep her informed! We must let her use our legs, direct them even. Do you understand? Do you understand what I'm talking about? Do you know how cruel it is to keep people in the dark?"

"For me," Douglas said, "it's a balancing act, between telling too much and telling too little. Too little can cripple, but so can too much."

"Well, one day you're going to have to tell me about Helen," Larry said, smiling his one-sided smile. "Just as, when we get home, we're going to tell mother about this afternoon. Right?"

"I'll tell you about Helen whenever you want. Or maybe she'll get a chance before too long to tell you about herself."

Douglas was aware of his son observing him in the darkness.

He feared it was another of those remarks which anticipated Edith's death. He drove slowly. The rain was slanting across his headlights, from the right, where the loch was, to the left, where the moor began.

Edith's Journal – 4

Larry keeps to the house these days. An idea or plan has occurred to him, I suspect, because he's not miserable any more but purposeful. He's told me about the arrest, how he and David, his new friend, suddenly saw they had to do something. Everything's being allowed to drift, he believes.

I'm not quite sure though what did happen. Each time he tells me, it's a slightly different story. First, the Americans shouted at them and they shouted back. Then the shouting was all on the American side, Larry and David just standing there. Then it was Larry and David who started it, incensed at drivers being held up, yet again, by a missile convoy. He doesn't seem aware of these inconsistencies and I don't draw them to his attention – I suppose because actually I'm quite proud of him. Even if I were to point them out, I doubt if he'd be able to know now what the truth is.

Douglas doesn't know what happened either, but whereas it doesn't bother me, it does him. All that matters to me is that something happened. Something was done. I don't think Douglas understands. He keeps going on about objective truth. But when this can't be ascertained, you can make of the truth what you will. Maybe that's how myths are born, myths of protest and rebellion and sacrifice and so on.

It's definitely got him thinking seriously. He seems almost delighted, actually. I'm so glad, because after he lost Ruth to "the American", as he calls him, he was very low, terribly agitated, no sooner in than out, out than in again. Not that he ever won Ruth from the American in the first place, I fear, though he'd have us believe otherwise. His accounts of the key moments in his life have always been so. As with the arrest, so with his love affairs. Vague, ambiguous. It used to annoy me, but not now. Now I take it to mean, not that he's a liar in any sense, but that he genuinely sees or feels events to be complex, shifting, strange.

He comes to me several times a day to talk. It's a great pleasure. I should also say a great relief, for it eases the pain. Good conversation as an antidote to pain: the healthy will find this hard to believe. But for people like me it is a great truth. Certain kinds of conversationalist can seem like healers.

Take this march, for instance, that is to take place in three weeks' time. Although neither Larry nor I are going on it, it excites us to think of the day. It's as if, like Christmas, it's a focus for the highest aspirations. Just discussing it is good for us, for the more we do so, the more we seem to be approaching an understanding of what we should do on the day, of how we should proclaim and conduct ourselves, while the others are marching, I mean, quietly and proudly, with their banners.

Sometimes I think that what we will see is that we should co-operate in some way, but then I think that probably we'll go our separate ways. We're not pacifists, as Douglas is, so we have many more options, we have to deliberate more.

How strange to be so excited about a day on which neither of us knows what he's going to do! All we know is what we're not going to do. We're not going to march and we're not going to hand out leaflets or pamphlets and we're not going to hector the crowd through loudspeakers. The one idea Larry has had is that he must do something which somehow exposes the horror which threatens us. An act of illuminating symbolism. But what this might be, he doesn't know. If I press him, he just laughs. We press each other to discover what we're going to do on the day and always end up laughing!

Sacrifice. The need for sacrifice. I have a feeling that that will be my theme. But what I will have to do to show it, make it manifest, I can't think.

So we wait for inspiration, my son and I, we wait to have it revealed what we must do on the day, laughing as we wait, joking, like schoolchildren, adolescents. I've rarely had such fun. On the day though it won't be fun. It will be beyond fun, terribly far from life at the moment. There can be no doubt about that.

Most of the time we're not together though. Then I know the pain is getting worse. The base of my spine seems to be under siege. Now from one direction, now from another, it is attacked, so that I have to move, or list, from side to side to ease it, and even that doesn't really help. It must look as if I have piles. Would it were as simple as that!

I've always dreaded pain in this particular region. The spine is the body's highway, isn't it? It connects all parts to the brain, the brain to all parts. Such horrors as incontinence can't be far away, I fear. To have to be told one has wet or fouled oneself. Not to know!

I'm helped a little actually by thinking of my body as a vast plain, myself as a fugitive seeking refuge from its weather. I can reach the point where I feel my body flowing away from me out into the darknesses of this plain. So the plain is my body but also my body flows out into it and away from me. For a moment or two then, when this happens, I am without pain. I enjoy a kind of exhilarating numbness.

To be hit by the pain again is like being hit, at some street corner, by a wind one thought one had escaped, a wind carrying the plague perhaps or a cold wind carrying fatal chills. That's not so far out actually, for there are hot pains and cold ones, each carrying its own message. I writhe in my chair, and, if no-one else is about, scream out. Screaming helps. Once I miscalculated though, screaming before Larry had left the house. He came to me so kindly and sat with me for hours. He knows he has the power to ease me. I hadn't wanted him to know it, but there it is, both husband and son bound to me, crippled by a cripple.

Larry and I have an agreement. When we discover what we must do on the day of the march, we'll tell each other. Bad to keep such things to oneself. Only occasionally, I'm glad to say, have I felt he's humouring me. I wouldn't blame him. What can a cripple be expected to do on any occasion? Oh well. Let the day of the march be fine and clear. A true spring day. On a day like that, I like to think, my pain may yet prove to be my ally.

VII

One evening about a week after Larry's arrest, a large black car approached the cottage. After a bright day, the dusk was soft, luminous. Watching from the living-room, Douglas and Edith thought how slowly the car was moving, as if it too was savouring the graciousness of dusk. When it stopped, four men in uniform got out, carefully brushing down their uniforms before opening the garden gate and walking – just this side of ceremonial slowness, Douglas thought – up the path to where a rectangle of light fell from the living-room window.

They saw that two of them were policemen, two from the American navy. They weren't talking; indeed it was as if they had done talking hours ago. Their knock when it came was peremptory, twice repeated.

For a moment after opening the door Douglas couldn't see anything at all. The men were standing back, out of the light. The better to see them, he stepped over the threshold, feeling as he did so that he was being looked over, checked.

A broad streak of orange light opened up in the western sky then, catching Douglas' attention. The foreground went into deeper shadow. Two of the men he could see in silhouette against it, two barely at all. To see more clearly, he raised a hand to his eyes, but it didn't make any difference. The orange light seemed both to be causing and framing his inability to handle the moment. He feared it might extend it indefinitely.

"Come in," he said at last, as though breaking a spell, "come in."

He didn't catch their ranks, only their names: Addison, McBride, Moretti, Goldberg. Silently they shook hands in the hall. Douglas led them into the living room where the fire, just stoked, was roaring and crackling, and Edith, a book on her lap, was looking at them over the top of her spectacles with ill-concealed suspicion.

One of the policemen went through the introductions again for the benefit of Edith. Douglas introduced her in turn. She made no attempt to extend a hand but simply nodded, soberly, four times. The officers sat down, caps on their knees.

"How can I help you, gentlemen?" Douglas asked.

The policeman who had done the introductions sat forwards, hands clasped, and began to speak. The others nodded, whether in agreement or to encourage him wasn't clear.

"I'm sure you can guess why we're here, Mr and Mrs Low. It's about Larry. But I don't want to suggest that we come to complain. Not at all! This is a peaceful visit. Contrary to popular opinion, we do pay peaceful visits, probably more peaceful ones than otherwise, in fact." The policeman paused, jerking his head forwards and upwards. "It is very likely that Larry will be found guilty of disturbing the peace, he and his young companion. Many are found guilty of it every day. It is not uncommon."

"Aren't you jumping the gun?" Douglas asked. "He's not been tried yet."

"Exactly," Edith said. "And, what's more, he doesn't think he's guilty."

"That may well be, one never knows," the policeman resumed awkwardly, "but what we've come here to say this evening is that we sincerely hope the incident hasn't soured your son against the police and our American friends here."

He fell silent. His companions were nodding again. Silent, he seemed at a loss, as if more was expected of him and he couldn't see what it was. The flesh of his cheeks trembled slightly.

"In this as in other matters we must keep a sense of proportion," one of the Americans said.

The policeman who had been speaking smiled broadly, as if this was just what he would have said had he been able to.

Attempts were being made to soften them up, Douglas could see.

From her wry look, Edith clearly thought so too. Their visitors were trying to ingratiate themselves – too pointedly however. Douglas wouldn't have been surprised had they been offered a free lunch or dinner at the base.

Suddenly Edith bowed her head, almost always a sign that she was bitter, angry, wrestling with herself. The silence deepened. It was as if each was waiting for the other to speak, remonstrate. The fire roared. Douglas forgot what had been said. To what exactly were they supposed to be responding? He sensed that the visitors were becoming embarrassed. Possibly they felt they had miscalculated in some way and were wondering how to regain the initiative. From the way they were sitting, bolt upright and looking straight ahead, they might have been trying to recall the exact details of some official brief.

Why should a minor infringement of the law be concerning them so? A scuffle at dusk on a cold highway have come to their attention? Beyond the suspicion that it hadn't – that they'd come not of their own accord but because they'd been sent – Douglas had no idea. He turned to Edith. With difficulty she had raised the knuckles of her right hand to her mouth. Briefly there was an odd sound, a kind of exasperated slavering.

"I don't understand your visit," she said. "I don't understand it at all. We must keep a sense of proportion – what kind of talk is that?"

The American smiled uneasily and rubbed his forehead.

"It surprises you?"

"Not so much that," Douglas said. "I just don't know what it means."

"A cripple, her husband and their son live in a quiet cottage," Edith broke in. "First of all, they come to your attention for some reason, then they're advised to keep a sense of proportion. It doesn't make any sense."

"Is Larry in?" the other American asked brightly, as if all it required for their visit to become intelligible was Larry's immediate appearance.

"Will that make any difference?" Douglas asked.

"He's young and enthusiastic," the American said. "We were all young once, of course, and can remember what it was like, how readily we took to things then. We get more resistant with the years, I think."

"Oh do we?" Edith was looking astonished.

A distant booming followed by a sudden gust of wind made them all look up. Sometimes the wind swept down the loch like this from the open sea. It always took Douglas and Edith by surprise. Always at first it seemed to be something else. They only knew it was the wind when the trees shook and moaned and the windows rattled, as they did now.

"There's been a gale warning," one of the policemen said. "It's the time of year for gales. March …"

"I can see we're just mystifying you," the other policeman said with an appeasing smile. "What's more, I can see why. Forgive us please. Let me try to be plain."

"That'd be much appreciated," Edith said. "Think of us as simple folk if you want. Be direct."

It was a difficult moment for Douglas as the policeman prepared to speak. He couldn't tell what was coming, found himself thinking of the worst: some revelation about himself and Helen – after all, hadn't they been photographed some time ago by someone in a missile convoy – or about Larry. Or both. If not a revelation, a warning, a warning probably so coded it would take them weeks to decipher. The need for some degree of secrecy sooner or later seemed to make it impossible for those in uniform to talk straight. Or was it the desire to keep people guessing, to make them wonder if they were guilty or not, and, if so, of what?

Breathing deeply, Douglas soon had the feeling that the policeman's words would pass on either side of him. He was aware of Edith struggling with the moment too, trying to discover some immunity to whatever was coming. To these youngish men in uniform, he realised, they must appear quite old.

"What we want to do is invite you, the three of you, to seminars. The Americans will be our hosts. Indeed it is their idea, and in my opinion a very good one. The initiative may have come from Washington, but it has been taken up very enthusiastically here. Notices will be going up all over the place. The idea is to allow people who are uneasy about the American presence to air their objections in open debate. We think this will be greatly preferable to the alternatives – noisy protests, violence, lawbreaking of various kinds."

Moretti, the American, took over now, with such enthusiasm it might all have been his idea.

"Yeah, you're cordially invited to come along. Young Larry especially. He seems like a young man with much to contribute. Not that we're saying we're open to change on essentials. For the sake of peace we could never do that. Obviously. But we would be happy to explain ourselves in debate. We have the feeling, you see, that our position isn't appreciated. Who knows, we may go some way towards persuading you of its rightness! All ranks will be present at the seminars, by the way, which will be led by education officers."

"Education officers?" Edith asked.

"Yeah. They're very much in demand on all sorts of subjects these days. I myself am attending a class on Shakespeare's history plays. So how do you feel? Do you think you might come along? Attendance is optional, of course, but we'll be very disappointed if you can't make it."

"I see," Douglas said.

"What do you see, sir?" Moretti asked.

"I get the picture," Douglas went on. "I must say, though, it's very enterprising of you. We'll certainly think it over."

"Sure, sure, I know you will. I wouldn't have expected any less of you. In the meantime ... here are three tickets, with our compliments."

He rose formally and, drawing a long white envelope from an inside pocket, handed it to Edith. Seeing she had difficulty in taking it, however, he offered it to Douglas instead. "With the compliments of the American Navy," Douglas read on the envelope, not knowing what to say, not managing any words at all, sitting, he feared, as though he had just been handed a summons.

"Can I offer you gentlemen anything?" he said at last. "Some tea, coffee, something stronger?"

"Is Larry in?" Moretti asked again.

"No," Edith said, "he's not in. But do stay for a refreshment."

"That's kind of you," one of the policemen said, "but we ought to be going. We've other calls to make."

The officers rose in unison, smiling, murmuring, holding their caps before them. In unison too they bowed to Edith, who nodded in response, attempting a smile.

Outside, there was a warm wind smelling of the sea. The streak of orange had gone. It was very dark.

The deputation went as quietly as it had come, with few words, an awkward politeness. Even the car was quiet, its engine drowned out by the wind. Douglas waved once, then went inside.

He found Edith shaking with silent laughter. To a stranger it might have seemed like pain, however, for her head was moving slowly up and down and she was wringing her hands. He stood behind her and placed his hands on her shoulders, thinking it was a long time since he had done such a thing. For a moment or two he managed to massage her, her neck, shoulders. Then, abruptly, he was laughing too.

The front door slamming and Larry calling from the hall interrupted them, but not for long. Edith was hooting now, Douglas hooting and cackling. "Can I share the joke?" Larry asked, coming into the room.

"Did you pass them?" Edith asked.

"Who?"

"Those jokers."

"Which jokers?"

"The ones that just left," Douglas said.

"I don't think I passed anyone."

"Four high-ranking officers," Douglas said. "They've just paid us a visit."

"Sit down and I'll tell you," Edith said, her voice suddenly harsh, her tone somewhere between sarcasm and despair. Spittle gathered about her mouth as she spoke and her gnarled hands, as though given by another for safekeeping, she held delicately before her. "The three of us are cordially invited to seminars at the American base where British and American nuclear policy will be discussed. The seminars will be led by American education officers. You especially are invited, Larry, because you are young and responsive and forthcoming. You can air your views in the civilised calm of a seminar room rather than indulge in civil disobedience outside, in the streets and lanes of our towns and cities. Nothing you say will make any difference though, has any chance of making them change their minds. But they may change ours! So you'd better cultivate a respectable debating manner. You'd better realise that the only respectable currency in all this is words, words and more words. Nothing else. Not sticks and stones, blows or bombs. Be a sophist, not a militant!"

She laughed mirthlessly for a few moments. Still standing behind her, Douglas placed his hands on her shoulders again. They were heaving, her hands clutching, unclutching.

Larry was nodding quietly.

"And if we should choose not to go?"

"In spite of their courtesy, I'm not sure we have that option," his mother replied. "I really don't think we have."

"Come to the front door," Douglas said after a silence, "come to the front door and smell the wind."

He pushed the wheelchair into the rectangle of light outside the front door. They faced the north-west, the quarter from which, with its warmth and its smell of the sea, the wind was blowing.

"Smells like spring to me," Larry said.

After lunch the next day Larry began to work on something in the back garden. It looked like a wooden hut, Douglas thought, but it could have been a boat. He worked with such urgency, so consumed by the task, that Douglas didn't ask him what it was, why he was doing it, why – if it was a hut – he hadn't asked permission. He didn't know where Larry had got the wood nor where, having got it, he had stored it. He didn't feel inclined to ask either; it might destroy his concentration, enrage him.

To begin with they watched from the living-room, sitting well back from the windows so that they could see without being seen. The wind that had risen the night before was still blowing. It was bending the pines and the birches, ruffling Larry's thin hair, making the clothes line jump as though electrified. There were occasional lulls, and in these Douglas and Edith could hear hammering and sawing which otherwise – Larry appearing to labour as in a kind of dumb show – the wind covered. Douglas had the fancy that it was the sawing that had arrested the wind, the hammering that kept it at bay. Both too seemed to give Larry authority. He knew what he was doing, had worked it out in advance and wouldn't stop until he had finished.

Edith said that it put her in mind of his early childhood when, for hours on end, he would work with blocks of wood, building walls and towers, bridges and battlements. Douglas thought that that might be it: building something

105

just for the hell of it or as a kind of therapy, a trick to reduce the burden of time and fate? Neither on the other hand; it was possibly neither. Larry would suddenly stop, for instance, look up and away as if he suspected he was being watched, take out a piece of paper and consult it, place it on the ground, weigh it down with a stone, rub his hands then with glee and astonishment. Didn't all that suggest someone with plans?

The wood was new, white mainly and sometimes catching the sun. Larry clearly enjoyed working with it, as well as just touching it, holding it. Douglas couldn't remember him doing carpentry before, let alone enjoying it. No doubt he had picked it up in his days with the forestry commission. Living wood and dead wood; trees and timber. Probably too that was where he had got the wood. And probably it was his intention, Douglas thought, that his parents should be bothered by such questions. Douglas wasn't going to ask them though. You didn't quiz an acrobat in mid-flight. You didn't do that; you didn't break such spells if you knew what was good for you.

What emerged at last from his labours was a hut. If neither Douglas nor Edith had any feeling of anti-climax, it was because the hut, though not quite finished, had been beautifully made. For three whole days – days of high wind and bright sun – Larry worked on it. Each night he covered it with tarpaulin, each morning lifted the tarpaulin off with something approaching reverence. But if the work enthralled him, it also exhausted him. At dinner he didn't mention it, and nor did his parents. Edith's view was that when it was completed to his satisfaction – then and only then – would he do so. Again she looked to his childhood for precedents. He had been a secretive child, she claimed, only owning up to his activities when he thought he had perfected them. Birdwatching, fishing, stamp collecting – his parents would be invited to admire only when he believed there was something to admire. So it would be

now, with the hut. When the last nail was in, the last sur-
face polished, he would come to them, overcome with pride
and excitement. So surely did Edith anticipate it, it was as if
she was hoping for a return to the simplicities of childhood.

The pretence that his parents weren't aware of what he
was doing went to ridiculous lengths. When it was lunch-
time, Douglas would go to the front door, wait for a pause
in the hammering, the sawing and the wind, and shout to
Larry, unseen behind the cottage, that his meal was in. And
when at table, sawdust in his hair and on his face, he would
refer, not to what he had just been doing, but to the book
he was reading at night. As if he was reading all day as well.
As if his life had become that of a student, a scholar.

On the fourth day, they saw him standing back, arms
folded, contemplating the hut, and knew that it was fin-
ished. Then it was as Edith had foretold, Larry even going
so far as to suggest that it had been built entirely for his
parents, entirely to their specifications, triumphant out-
come of some long cherished family dream.

Soon afterwards Douglas pushed Edith out into the
garden to see it. Birds were singing, the air was warm, and
there was a pleasant smell of new wood. He pushed the
wheelchair slowly round the hut, leaving it to Edith to make
comments, congratulate Larry on his achievement (she had
always been much better at this sort of thing than he). Then
Larry opened the door of the hut and invited them to look
inside. There was a raftered roof, four small windows and a
raised wooden floor on which he had laid a rug.

"The door is broad enough for your chair," Larry said,
"should you ever want to sit inside. I'm going to make a
ramp for it."

Edith nodded vigorously, as if it was very likely that in
the coming weeks she would want to do this.

While Larry took charge of the wheelchair, Douglas
stepped into the hut. The smell of new wood was very
strong, and it was warm and still. On the edge of the stillness

he could hear Edith and Larry murmuring. Perhaps Edith was again praising her son's handiwork, he, bent low over the wheelchair, thanking her. Or perhaps he was now confessing that he had built the hut entirely for her. A retreat for meditation. It struck Douglas that he could build him a new observatory, bigger than the present one and warmer. One hut for the mother, one for the father.

Nothing had been said about its purpose. For two days, in fact, Larry didn't go near it. Then Douglas saw him attaching a lock to it, then, later in the day, entering with books, files and what looked like manuals. He stayed for an hour or so and when he emerged looked very thoughtful. Next he took some planks of wood in with him and again there were sounds of sawing, hammering, planing. Sometimes he worked with the door open, sometimes with it shut, and sometimes he worked so vigorously the hut shook.

One day Edith asked him what it was for.

"It's a workshop I've made for myself out there. Soon I'll be building something in it. I'm not sure yet what form it'll take. I'll show you when I'm finished – if I'm pleased with it. As with the hut. I hope you understand."

His plans seemed to excite him, Douglas thought, but also to disconcert him. He said of course they understood.

"How long will it take?" Edith asked.

"Well, I have to have it finished by a particular date."

"What date is that?" Douglas asked.

"The date of the march," Larry replied. "The date of the march." He looked from one parent to the other, not so much to scrutinise as to offer himself for scrutiny.

"You need it for the march?" Edith enquired.

"Not so much for the march as on the day of it."

"I need something for the day of the march too," Edith said with a kind of studied remoteness, "only I can't think what."

Larry looked at his mother sympathetically.

"You're not too keen on marches, are you?"

"It's more than just that I can't march. We've reached the stage when it isn't enough, I think."

"I agree," Larry said, nodding, looking away. "That's my feeling exactly."

"Can you be more explicit?" Douglas asked. "What's wrong with a march?"

"Nobody notices them any more. They're old hat. Extreme situations demand extreme responses," Larry said.

Edith was nodding.

"Yes: we owe it to ourselves not to become old fashioned, dear."

"But what else do you propose?" Douglas asked. "Our powers are not unlimited."

"That's surely up to the individual," Larry said quietly. "I'll be working on my plan, quite soon, trying to make something of it, and mother ..."

"Well, hold on," Edith said. "What options are open to cripples? To sit here meditating for hours on end? To wheel myself from door to door, haranguing?"

There was a silence before she spoke again, and but for her hands, clutching and unclutching like some creature of the sea-bed, she might almost have been amused.

"Not to remember that my options are severely limited gets me nowhere."

"Mother," Larry said, reaching out a hand.

"It's true. A simple fact."

"You could come with me," Douglas said. "Along the loch-side for four miles and into the town. There'll be speeches."

"I'm sorry, Douglas, but you make it sound futile." She was grinning as she did when in pain.

"You could join up with me," Larry said. "I could do with a hand."

"But I couldn't give you one; I don't have one: I'm a cripple! Why can't you see that!? Anyway, you've not told me what you're going to do."

"I could let you know. When it's developed a bit further, I could let you know."

"Alright. If I can't see what I'm called upon to do – by God, if you like – and think that this means I've no contribution to make, you can tell me. I'll consider it."

"I can't see what'd be more effective than a march," Douglas said, speaking quickly, as if fearful of interruption. "I can't even see what more you could do, effective or not. Short of violence, of course, but that's unacceptable, I think we all agree."

Larry lifted his hands as though for silence. He was smiling. The building of the hut and now the undisclosed project in it had made him proud. His manner was assured, the skin of his face appeared tighter, finer. He took his time before speaking.

"I think that what I'm planning to do will be an advance on marches. It doesn't involve violence, though it speaks of it, inevitably."

"Can you be any clearer?" Edith asked.

"I'll try. What I want to do … is attempt to remind people, much more vividly than a march ever could, of this one fact: that nuclear violence is terminal, that there will be no getting on with life after it's over. Our situation is uniquely terrible. I want to try and dramatise this. Marches don't do it, never did do it, not even in the sixties. Apart from the banners, they're all the same. I hate their passivity. I think that what they show is not the power of people before governments, but their helplessness."

"So you're going to appear dressed up as a skeleton," Douglas said, more sarcastically than he had intended. "It's a skeleton you're making in the hut."

"That would be old hat too," Larry replied. "There's nothing new about effigies."

"Yes," Edith said, "It would only work, ah … if you were to become a skeleton before their very eyes."

"Before whose very eyes?" Douglas asked.

"Everyone's. Those marching, those watching from the roadside, on the television ... Yes, everyone. A global audience. This is the age of global audiences."

She was smiling too now, not a smile like Larry's, not assured and composed like that, but startled rather, excited, a smile as of discovery, not consolidation. It irked Douglas that they were both smiling; less and less could he see anything to smile about. They cared so little about marches they didn't even want to hear why he believed in them, saw them as enduringly relevant, not modish at all.

He wondered if he could manage a defence. He stood up, more to secure a window against the cold windy day actually than to address them. But he was determined to address them; he believed there were important points to make. Immediately he found though that he wasn't able to be as passionate in defence of marches as they were against them. Edith didn't look at him – not unusual, for it pained her to turn her head – but nor did Larry. Yes: they were more ardent in their secretiveness than he in his openness – more dignified, too.

"I've never pretended," he began, "that marches are momentous in their effects. But what is? The only alternatives, I honestly believe, are nothing at all or acts ... probably too close to violence."

"In my opinion, marches are almost indistinguishable from nothing," Larry said.

Not to seem absurd, standing where he was with so little to say, Douglas moved Edith over to the window, where there was a little sunshine. She thanked him, going along with the pretence.

"So long as people hold back from marches, they won't be effective," he went on, standing by the window with his hands on the back of the wheelchair. "Too few go on them: that's the trouble. Imagine marches a hundred times bigger. Imagine this Easter march with a million people.

Imagine that. Then you'd see how effective they can be. You can't judge them as they are."

"But there used to be bigger marches," Edith said, "and the reason they got smaller was precisely because they weren't effective."

"Exactly," Larry said.

Douglas sat down but kept a hand on the wheelchair. He was becoming a little breathless, he feared, and hoped it wasn't apparent. He tried to breathe deeply. It helped, he had found, if when you were doing so, you looked at something pleasant. He looked out of the window therefore at the wind in the trees and the tall grasses. The way the wind could flatten the grasses and turn them grey – this struck him particularly. As if colour was not of the world but simply visited it.

Soon he became aware of two rhythms, an involuntary one, which seemed wrong, unhealthy, and the one he was trying to impose on it, a rhythm of assuaging and ideal regularity. It wasn't a matter of hoping for the best, he now thought, but of working for it. And indeed, even as he thought this, he seemed to be achieving it, the tight breathing that had threatened his upper chest beginning to give way before a richer respiration arising from below, from depths he was happy to believe were his. His head cleared too, all manner of distractions he hadn't been aware of as such slipping away, amongst them the idea that if he didn't persuade Edith and Larry of the importance of marches he had failed, and failed in some fundamental way.

"We must agree to differ," he said at last quietly. "I'll march, you two … make your own arrangements."

"Do you want me to tell you what I'm hoping to do?" Larry suddenly asked.

"You never were much good at keeping secrets," Edith said. "All right, tell us."

"What I'm aiming to do … is present people with a nuclear explosion in miniature. No violence is intended and none will be done. In the hut … are the beginnings of a boat. It'll be flat, rather like a raft, and powered by a small engine. Not so flat though that it runs a risk of sinking. When the march is passing the base, I'll set this boat off, across the loch and towards the base. About eighty yards from the base, it'll blow up – a small bomb, but the explosion will be very loud. Slowly into the Easter sky then a mushroom cloud will rise. It will be very black, its underside spinning, fulminating. Symbol of death, universal destruction. Everyone will hear the explosion and everyone will turn to the cloud. Most probably, in fact, the march will stop. There will be terror at first, I realise, but that can't be helped. I think actually that for the moment to strike home there has to be terror."

He paused for a moment.

"It'll not be easy of course, not at all. It's going to require such co-ordination. The engine will have to start immediately, not stall; it'll have to get the boat to the right spot at the right time; and, when the boat gets there, the explosion will have to occur. Needless to say, it's giving me nightmares. But oh I can hear it now, the explosion, echoing around the low hills! And at the same time the cloud, expanding over the loch, blotting out the sun – an eclipse in miniature, and with all the terror, awe eclipses inspire!"

He paused again.

"Another thing. I'll have to find a place from which to launch the raft. And I'll have to have it hidden before that. I'll also have to launch it when no one is looking. You can see why I'm thinking of a helper."

Most of the way through Larry's explanation Edith had been laughing silently. Her shoulders were heaving, Douglas could see. This woman whose will was indistinguishable sometimes from the pain which inspired it was entirely convulsed. Her hands, as in an attempt at applause, made several times to rise from her lap, but fell back, whether from pain or mirth – or both – wasn't clear.

"What a wonderful idea!" she said at last in a cracked voice. "How long did it take you to think that up? Or did it come just in a flash?"

"That's it – a flash!" Larry was smiling triumphantly.

"I hope that's how it'll be with me," Edith said. "One gets so tired of thinking. So very tired."

"Have faith," Larry said. "You'll have your vision too."

"I fear I'll have to humble myself before that happens. That won't be easy."

There was a silence. Douglas was on his feet again. He was the obvious helper for Larry, he knew, but he was reluctant to offer himself. Helen would be a better choice, for she didn't think much of marches either, she too yearned for something different. If he could find a way of involving her without Edith becoming suspicious, he would do so. They would be an effective couple, Larry and Helen.

His will not to betray the march was strong. He thought of the loch on the days when it was flat calm, mirror for hills, trees and sunlight. It seemed to speak of the spirit in which they should march. Why get caught up with Larry, find himself required to crouch in undergrowth by the shore, worry about a craft with a small explosive device, not to mention about his son, author of the whole thing? As it was, he feared, he wouldn't be able to march as he wanted to, in a truly steadfast spirit. Larry and Edith and Helen had seen to that.

"Give me time to think it over," he said, aware that his wife and son were looking at him. "I'll let you know."

He had hoped to sound firmly principled, but suspected he seemed merely displeased, peevish even. He shrugged his shoulders.

Edith's Journal – 5

I haven't been able to sleep tonight because of the pain. Could it have been any worse if I hadn't taken any pills at all? As it is, I've taken one more than usual. I groan into my pillow, not to disturb Douglas. Sometimes he groans too, in his sleep. Waking groans, sleeping groans. Arias of a kind, you could say.

He's used to me having the light on. He's never allowed me to feel that anything I do at night out of my discomfort – reading, writing, listening to my little radio, writhing, cursing – disturbs him. Even when I wake crying from a nightmare (the pills definitely make these worse) and go on crying, from the pain, he'll come to my bedside as though it's a privilege.

I'd like to wake him now, just to talk, but I won't. I'd only wake him if it was absolutely necessary, if something absolutely had to be done for me that I couldn't do myself. Or – yes – if his breathing was bad, shallow, irregular. That was his request after his heart attack, actually: not to be allowed to die in his sleep, without saying goodbye. To be wakened for last words. Mortus interruptus. One of his sweetest notions but one of his craziest. Nonetheless I have a stick hanging from the back of my bed to prod him with in the event. We both seem to believe in the pact even although I could no more grasp the stick and prod him with it than fly in the air.

The window is open slightly, the curtains gently moving. There must be a slight breeze. I can smell the new wood from Larry's hut. The night which belongs to invalids and lovers makes me very responsive to smells. I can picture the hut, proudly locked against intruders, inside it the raft, the raft of destiny. Saturday, April the thirteenth. He's told me he can't see beyond that day; time stops for him then. I understand perfectly, for it's the same for me, even although I don't yet know what I'll be doing.

Sometimes I think I'll just position myself so that I can see the raft go out into the middle of the loch and explode. High up, there are many vantage points. To see it explode so close to the base – within hailing distance, mocking distance – would be great, a kind of honour, unforgettable.

And maybe I can will success for him. Maybe the concentration of a soul is not in vain. Vain to think it may be. The spirit's energies, the cleaving will.

Still though I feel I'll be doing my own thing. It's on the tip of my tongue. The very verge. God is teasing me: a test of faith. Children of destiny, Larry and I. At least not dupes. Not that.

Earlier in the night, before I took up this journal again, I lay with my right arm dangling out of the bed. I felt as if I was reaching out to Douglas, across the space between the beds, cripple to sleeper. Just sometimes, you see, the pain seems to refine my limbs, not numb them, to make them antennae. I have the sense that I can cross spaces. As if to compensate for my terrible immobility, cross spaces: I imagine it anyway and to imagine something is just about to do it. The imagination isn't bound by space and time as this body is or this room in which it suffers.

Tonight I felt it very powerfully, felt I was stroking Douglas' brow, holding his hands, touching his neck, felt I was responsible for the calmness of his breathing, the health and even grandeur of his dreams. Involuntarily, so it seemed, I spoke a few words to him, his name, apologies, promises, endearments. Emollients into sleep's darkness. Briefly all across the plain then the pain fled to the periphery. But came back almost immediately, violently, as before a wind. How vindictive it sometimes seems to be! After the sense of union – reaching Douglas even in his sleep, consoling and even loving him there – the sense that I can neither reach nor be reached. The pain does with me what it wills; I have the illusion of will merely. I'm a ball of darkness rolling about in the darkness.

If I die naturally, rather than implore Douglas to give me an overdose – not inconceivable – it'll surely be because the demon pain has grown tired of visiting me and wants to try others, unpractised and untutored souls, spoilt by health, over-confident. (Too much to hope it can feel pity.

If it could, it wouldn't be itself, would it?) Or because I've run out of strategies, simply that.

At one point Larry went to the lavatory – about 3 a.m. I think it was. Considerately he tip-toed past our door, which is always slightly ajar. I was strongly tempted to call out to him. I fancied actually that he paused, tempted to call in. He isn't sleeping so well at the moment. No wonder. He worries about the raft, the explosive device, the whole question of timing. So many things could go wrong. The worst, he tells me, is that the device could blow up in his face, killing him. He assures me it's highly unlikely, a chance in ten million. I like to think his mention of it was just bravado, the inevitable manliness, the sweet boast of a proud son. His main fear, a realistic one, is that the raft will sink, the explosive device with it. He dreads the humiliation of this even more than that of an abortive explosion – a kindergarten pop and puff, as he calls it.

Another anxiety concerns his father. Will he agree to help or not? If not, who will? I suggest David, but he shakes his head. Too unreliable apparently.

He wants to be able to put the raft in the water and set it off towards the base without being seen. For this, he needs a look-out who'll give a signal. When there is a gap in the march, a clearing (there always are, he needn't worry), a sign or signal. I'd do it myself, needless to say, but a cripple in the road giving signals from her wheelchair would be very conspicuous.

I'm inclined to think that Douglas will eventually agree. He knows as well as I do that for Larry to be caught would be serious, what with the recent arrest and so on. A prison sentence probably. My hunch is that his paternal feelings will overcome his principles. Larry is banking on it too, I know, but he's not so confident. He'll have a lot of explaining to do if he refuses, and could he face that? Could he? He'd also better take part sincerely, for otherwise Larry's judgement might be affected. I'll be telling him so.

117

The thought of the march, or of the day of it, has us all on the boil, but we boil in different ways. We are three such different people.

Some kind of celebration, I believe, will be called for if it all goes off perfectly, if the explosion takes place exactly when and where it should and if its effects are precisely as Larry believes they can be. A renewal of the nuclear wound, awe, consternation, panic, vision. I can't think of a celebration though. Truly I can see nothing beyond the day. It's as if I've given myself over to the idea that we'll be staging the end of the world, dramatising it. Is that why I see nothing beyond? Because there is nothing beyond the end of the world?

I tell myself this is to confuse fact with fiction, the world with the stage, but it doesn't make any difference. Beyond Saturday, April the thirteenth, all is darkness, silence. God help me but I've never had such a feeling before. It concentrates the mind wonderfully. My God it does. Perhaps it'll drive out the pain? Not much sign of that at the moment. Much more of this and it'll take me hours to get going today. On the thirteenth, I can only pray, it won't be so.

Towards dawn it rains. I'm not so much aware of it starting as of it having been raining, very gently, for some time. It is the sound of mild spring rain irrigating the land. I welcome it, recognise it as something I've always known. So long as there is an earth to irrigate, it will be there, heaven sent apparently.

Not fully awake, I allow myself the fancy that if it were to fall on me, if I were lying in a calm field somewhere and it were to fall on me, I would be restored. In fact when Douglas wakens, which should be quite soon, I'll ask him to massage me, my legs especially. It won't ease the pain really but it can remind me that having legs was once other than this.

VIII

The way sleep could change him, his mood and beliefs even, had always fascinated Douglas. Recently it had been more apparent than ever. It had got so that he occasionally flirted with the idea that he was two people, two temperaments. In sleep he could move from the one to the other. The journey had no stages and he would never know when it was going to happen. The being who had gone to sleep was not always the one who woke up, and, when it was, he sometimes had to admit to a sense of disappointment: sleep had not modified or extended him this time, had not cast him up on a new shore.

How he saw it, frailty or strength, was itself subject to change, instance of the phenomenon itself. If it suggested an arbitrariness in him, an absence of core or nucleus, this didn't trouble him for it seemed to be a condition of freedom. He would not be ground down in weariness of himself. He could depend on this shedding of skins. With a few exceptions, his beliefs were open to change apparently. In sleep he could be separated from them, they could be cut loose, as though to lodge themselves in another. Sleep, migration, metamorphosis.

He could fall asleep longing for Helen and wake with the suspicion that she didn't matter that much to him any more. Or go to sleep feeling dark about her but wake with the sense that somehow during the night she had moved closer to him. He'd think he couldn't cope with Edith any more but then that he could, he longed to, it was essential to him. He didn't respect Larry and would send him away for the good of his soul; he respected him very much and would strive to keep him at home. He was becoming an adventurer; he was becoming a recluse. Life with Helen, give or take an obvious fact or two, would be much like life with Edith; it would be utterly different.

Sometimes he thought that what he was doing was paying for his adultery. He was a husband and a lover; he had loved two women. If you were with neither exclusively, however, were you with either at all? Were you anywhere? The fluidity of his being then could seem like evaporation, dissolution.

For weeks the two women had been talking the same kind of language, the quasi-philosophical language of illumination and disclosure. They said how much they envied Larry his discovery of a higher purpose for the day. It hadn't yet been revealed to them what they should do. They hadn't had an inspiration. It was a matter of faith, of waiting. And so on.

Both found Douglas' position unacceptable, beneath notice even. He had virtually stopped talking to them about it, his commitment to the march obviously as irritating to them as their elevated and soulful uncertainty was to him.

Gradually, however, he had been approaching the view that it was he who should be Larry's helper. It would mean not marching, he knew, and that pained him; but the thought of his son struggling on his own or with an unreliable helper pained him more. It might be what he would have to do.

But then, one morning, with spring approaching, he woke with a clear and vigorous mind. He saw what he should do. Not an insight which would change either, he was sure; it would be proof against time and sleep.

He would march on his own, on the way perhaps striking up a few acquaintanceships. Afterwards he would listen to the speeches in the square, applauding if he felt like it. Then he would go for a drink in the Merchantman's

Arms, a pint or two. Edith could do what she liked. He would park her where she wanted to be parked. Collect her when the march was over.

And Helen? It was she who would be Larry's helper! Though excitable under pressure, with a tendency to panic, she would do it. They could rehearse together, minimising the possibility of error and mischance. It would be up to them. His business was the march. One mind through and through, and, afterwards, faithful to the memory.

He rang Helen about it and she agreed immediately. He had made her day, she said. They would start rehearsals as soon as possible. They would work towards perfection on the shore. He let her talk on, excited gratitude, hyperbole and worse. At least now she wouldn't march in mockery.

He mentioned it to Larry. He too was excited. To spare Edith's feelings, he quickly said, he would say that Helen was his friend rather than Douglas'. Douglas would be released to indulge in the "passive protest" of the march and Edith …

"I'm not sure about her," Douglas said.

"What d'you mean? There's nothing really she can do. Except sit on a high place and meditate."

"Maybe. But it's not what she would have done had she been able …"

"How d'you know? Maybe it's exactly what she would have done."

"We just can't know. But it saddens me – that it's her only option."

"It's not as if she's making tea and handing out sandwiches …"

"Do you know anything about meditation?" Douglas asked bluntly.

"No. Do you?"

"Not really."

Edith had been practising meditation for about ten years, but Douglas had to admit he was still vague about it. He couldn't have talked on the subject for five minutes. He had tended to classify it, he suspected, with herbal remedies and homeopathy, to which occasionally Edith had turned in her pain. If he had given it any thought at all, it had been condescendingly. Trances, detachment, equilibrium: all gained at the expense of humour. He was ashamed.

Also now he felt challenged. How might meditation be a significant alternative to marching on Saturday, April 13th? What might it mean to claim this? He believed he ought to try and explain it to Larry, obsessed, he thought, with his raft, his explosive device, his nuclear cloud.

He might find, of course, that Larry knew more about meditation than he did – he could hardly know less. If so, Douglas knew less about Larry than he ought to, and less than he thought he had. Wife and son. It wasn't too late to understand them better. It almost seemed it was, though, what with the march imminent, Helen beckoning, Edith's restlessness.

"Meditation," he ventured gravely, "is an art your mother has been practising for years. I can't say I've followed her in it, but each has his own remedies."

"And each his own pain," Larry said, looking away.

Larry had done many things in his twenty-five years. Few of his interests or passions had lasted however. Douglas had a sense suddenly that one of these might have been meditation. Edith could have inspired him to try it, remedy for depression, disappointment in love, boredom. Or he could have started it himself, without her knowing, tried it for a month or two, given up.

He looked at his son anxiously, hoping he wasn't going to be exposed, lectured.

"Meditation is triumphantly sustained controlled breathing," Larry began in a level voice. "If it's an art, as you say, it's the art of controlled breathing. You breathe with the universe; it's mystical. If you'd had the art all your adult life, you'd not have had your heart attack. D'you know that? You keep yourself easy now by breathing well. You do. I've seen you at it. It's admirable."

"True enough, I try that."

"Well, imagine that what you do in snatches, clauses, mother does in paragraphs and entire chapters. That's the sort of triumph it is."

"No doubt. I like to think so."

The clamour and chaos in his chest that morning, his heart protesting. The haggard and irritable and demeaning days he had passed beforehand. Deadly sweats. On the day itself, the most deadly sweat of all. You'd have thought a tank was bursting.

He smiled quickly, as if ashamed, caught out in a weakness. He hadn't looked after himself in those days; wouldn't have known what it was to do so really. He hadn't gone on marches either. Now he did both and permitted himself the thought that there was probably some connection. For heart's ease, it seemed, and even in darkness you had to pay certain attentions to the world.

"You'll have to practise a lot, you realise," he said, "the two of you."

"That's for certain! It'll give me a chance to get to know her. She can't help me in a venture like this unless we know and trust each other." He grinned, looking at his father directly.

"She can be excitable but she can also be cool."

"Fine," Larry said. "Let's just say that she can do … what mother would probably have done had she been able."

Douglas turned aside. The sense that he was about to see with great vividness what it would have been like to be married to Helen was upon him. Or what it would have been like had Edith not become crippled all those years ago. Such visions had been promised before but never realised. Now for some reason he thought they were going to be, one or the other, both. He felt very alert, was straining actually, perspiring. To what end though? To what end such knowledge?

It passed again, however – perhaps would always pass. He turned back to Larry who, the way he had reached out a hand to him, might have thought his father was becoming ill again.

"It's O.K.," Douglas said. "I'm O.K."

Not far from the town the coast road went through a series of S bends. For quarter of a mile in wet or misty conditions motorists could feel that they'd been claimed by a bad stretch of road. On Saturday, April 13th, the march was to pass this way. (With gaps or pauses between the groups or contingents, it might seem – to someone watching from a bank – like a succession of small marches rather than one long one; but to the marchers there would be a strong sense of unity.) On the left as the town was approached there was a row of beech trees; they followed the curve of the road, actually the curve of the coast. Behind them was a rocky promontory. Here, because it was the spot from which Larry planned to launch his raft, Douglas had arranged to meet Helen. She had said on the phone that she knew it well: everything conspired to make it the most dramatic part of the coast, in her opinion.

A bright, windy day, with high white clouds, curdled, crenellated, a fine pageant of sky moving from the north west to the south. Now and then reflections of the clouds showed briefly on the surface of the loch, fragmented, trembling.

Rounding a bend, Douglas and Larry saw Helen moving in dappled sunlight by the beech trees, a neat figure in a belted brown raincoat. She was scrutinising the spot apparently, as for flaws, imperfections, walking backwards and forwards with strict steps, so absorbed in her task she barely registered their approach. Only when Douglas drove off the road and parked under one of the trees did she look up and saunter towards them, out of the dappled area into one of brightness, right hand raised to shade her eyes.

Larry was grinning. He said how smart she looked. He couldn't go wrong with a partner like that. How long did Douglas say he'd known her? He was first out of the car then to greet her, shaking her hand ceremoniously, pumping it.

"Yes, this is the spot. It's the only possible one. I think of it most of the time. I know all the rocks, the branches .... It's in my head, here." He tapped his head, still grinning.

"It certainly seems ideal," Helen said. "You can even hear larks – listen, when the wind drops and there's no traffic."

Larry made a sweeping gesture with his right arm, as of ownership or intended ownership. Then, with the exaggeratedly strict and lengthened stride of one measuring out a cricket pitch, he walked off down the road, head rolling, arms lifted slightly from his sides. He went round one corner and then, where the road doubled back on itself, a second. Then he stopped and stood very still.

"What's he doing?" Helen asked.

"I don't know. He's always been one for measurements. As if in measurements is safety."

They stood and watched him returning, still with the same exaggerated stride, eyes half shut.

"A hundred and eighty two yards," he said, "a hundred and eighty two yards from here to the second corner. I reckon it'll take them about three minutes to do it."

He was breathing heavily, hands on hips.

"I don't think I'll be able to see the second corner from my place on the shore. And I can't afford to wait until they get to the first corner; I might be seen. I'm hoping for a gap between groups, you see. I'll launch the raft when this part of the road is clear. It's the only safe way. That means though that there will have to be someone signalling from the second corner to someone at the first. I'll take my cue from the person at the first. I know I can see him from the shore."

Douglas and Helen said nothing. They might have been waiting until it became interesting or comprehensible before they responded.

"Could we try it then?" Larry went on, clenching his right hand and punching it into his left. "Dad at the second corner, Helen at the first. I know that, on the day, you'll be marching, Dad, but just for the moment ..."

"Anything to oblige," Douglas said.

"You hold your right arm up – like this – and, when the way is clear, you drop it. It'll be the signal. O.K.?"

Helen nodded, lifting and dropping her right arm obediently. Douglas said nothing, thinking that on the day he ought to be far back from the explosion or well in advance of it, not here by the beech trees sensing or even seeing the crouched figure of his son amongst the rocks. He pictured the raft exploding in his face, killing him and some of the marchers. Thick black smoke would cover the bodies and block out the sun but there would be photographs nonetheless in the papers the next day. After that the spot would be silent forever in his imagination. Driving past it would be like losing consciousness and walking past it impossible. Edith would ask to be brought to it however, in all weathers sitting in her wheelchair under the beech trees, not so much in vigil as in expiation, haggard and astounded until death took her.

Larry went off through the trees, ducking to avoid branches, climbed down a bank to the shore and made his way along a rocky promontory. There, where a bush grew, he knelt down, seemed to examine the water.

After a few moments he stood up, slowly and reflectively, went round the back of the bush and, as if it was a hut of some kind, entered it. They heard him call out to them then, asking them to go along the road to their positions.

Of all Larry's projects over the years, Douglas thought, this was the craziest. Heroic maybe but the craziest;

certainly the most dangerous. He asked Helen what she thought of it, now that they were here, by the shore, the American base in sight, its ceaseless and impenetrable busyness coming and going on the wind even as he spoke and she answered.

"I still think it's a great idea," she said, slipping her arm through his and, as though to comfort him, matching her stride to his. "Daring, but with such rightness. You mustn't try to stop him."

"I couldn't possibly. He can do what he likes. So can you. So can I. So can Edith."

"I felt honoured to be asked, actually," Helen said.

"I'm glad. I'll have to be far off, though, when he launches the thing ..."

"He'll be needing two helpers though. He said so."

"I know, I heard him, but I'll not be one of them."

"That's that then," Helen said brightly.

They walked in silence to the first corner, where they parted without a word, Douglas going on to the second corner, shambling a little as he went. It was as though, he thought, they were rehearsing, not just the moves for Saturday 13th, but the feelings and passions as well. Almost certainly there would be fear, anger, estrangement. And suddenly, as out of these feelings and passions, he had a desire to mock.

"Helen," he shouted, "shouldn't you be standing to attention or something?"

"Raise your right arm," she shouted back, "and, when you drop it, I'll drop mine."

Already a form, a ritual, seemed to have been established, clear enough and insistent enough to restrain Douglas from further mockery. Positioning, timing, vigilance, signalling: on such details Larry's fate clearly depended.

He thought that if he were to stand in for the second helper too many times he might find it difficult to back out. Acting the part might make him covet it. The part

127

might claim him. He might see the necessity of it and of the project of which it was a part.

There were no such necessities and urgencies in the case of the march. You started in one place and ended in another, where there were speeches. What was wrong with that though? Or in his sixties was he still to know himself? Was he a pacifist or not? Should he perhaps not have come today at all?

After a long silence, Douglas dropped his arm, Helen hers too. Abruptly Larry stood up from his place among the rocks and waved a red handkerchief. He was shouting something, but it was broken up by the wind and borne away behind him, across the loch. Briefly there was a dumb show, Larry mouthing wildly behind the wind's mask, isolated for a few moments with his desperate convictions, author of his fate but daunted, driven, Helen waving back to him but as though to calm him merely.

Then she trotted down the road to meet him, Larry coming up through the trees with a sort of embattled urgency, arms waving, head rolling. They conferred in the middle of the road, gesturing, laughing, as though encouraged by the dappled light about them. Douglas strolled towards them, stopping not because he felt it wasn't his business but because he wanted to see how they looked together. Just that. He thought they looked fine, animated, purposeful, in command. Possible to envy them. Undesirable though.

"Everything O.K.?" he asked, sauntering up.

They looked past him, he thought, rather than at him.

"I didn't see Helen clearly at the first corner," Larry complained, "not at all clearly. It's essential that I do however, not just for timing but for morale. I'd like her to stand four or five yards back therefore, to take her cue there from whoever's at the second corner."

"I'm sorry there are these complications," Douglas said.

Again they seemed to look past him.

"I think I ought to say," Douglas began, "that if you absolutely can't find a second helper, I won't see you stuck."

"That's good of you." Larry spoke with a kind of pedantic brightness. "I appreciate it. There are some though who wouldn't have any objections on principle."

"True," Douglas said.

"I might even advertise."

"How could you do that without giving yourself away?"

"Easy."

"Would you have the time though?"

"The time?"

"To advertise?"

"Why not?"

Douglas looked over at Helen, standing some ten yards away, and found that she was looking at him, her eyes affectionate and cheerful but cautionary. Over Larry's head, so to speak, a look of love. He realised that he wanted Larry to be aware of it, yet not too directly, for then he might give in to discontent, mockery.

"Come and see where I'll be launching it from."

Although he spoke abruptly, it was not so much an order as an invitation to come and approve, Douglas felt.

Stooping, Douglas behind Helen, they followed Larry through the trees and down to the shore, occasional branches whipping back into their faces. On the shore, Larry offered Helen his hand which gratefully for ten yards or so over the worst of the rocks she took, holding it up and out from her as though they were approaching a dance floor. To Douglas, it seemed like an instant of elaborate flirtation, the leader led as much as leading. Why not, if they were to be partners together and in danger too? Hadn't they earned the right? He commended them in his heart.

Out from the trees, the air was colder, saltier. They looked across the water. The base seemed about three hundred yards away, Douglas thought – hard to tell though, what with the waves and the dancing light. The usual sounds of activity came and went on the wind: commands, emissions, as of steam, gas, hammering, rolling, dragging, the odd piercing whistle. They listened carefully, as if, with patience, purposes might be divined in this clamour across the water. Douglas realised he had been hearing such sounds for a long time, at all times of the day and night, always scrambled and virtually meaningless but today, for some reason, appearing to be about to come together in momentous significance to disturb and arrest them as they stood on the rocky promontory from which, sideways rather than upwards, the solitary bush grew.

"My bush and my protection," Larry said, gesturing. "I hope it won't be so choppy on the day though. It'll make aiming difficult. And the raft may take on water."

"The base seems so far away," Helen said, "like a photograph of a very strange place, a place where all the customs are different. I suppose a strong swimmer could reach it quite quickly though, even through these white horses."

Larry was gazing at the base with a kind of defiant intentness and uncertainty. Images of defeat and failure, farce and fiasco, were probably occurring to him, his father thought. He had always chosen ventures where failure was as spectacular as success, humiliation as profound as triumph. It was the reason why his life, in spite of its manifest absurdities and indignities, had elements of the heroic almost. The thought astonished Douglas. On the one side farce, on the other the heroic.

"It wouldn't be possible to test it somewhere? On a quieter loch to give it a trial run?"

"No chance. Absolutely not. I haven't time to make another raft, not to mention fix up another explosive device. Nor the money either. No ... we'll just have to pray for inspiration and calm conditions." When he spoke again, it was much more quietly. "There comes a point when you can't do any more. You're as prepared as you'll ever be. That's where I am now. You learn how strange it is to wait, though. It's very strange …"

"You know," Helen said, taking his arm, "I truly believe we're going to startle everyone in the grandest manner. The march will stop and even your father will raise his eyes to heaven."

"Would it be one of your intentions, by any chance, to shock us so deeply we can't see the point of resuming the march?" Douglas asked, uncertain whether he was trying to rebuke his son or pay him tribute.

"I want the whole damned world to sit up," Larry said. "There will be nothing to cap it."

"I mightn't have done anything at all, you know, if I hadn't met you," Helen said. "I'm very grateful."

"Mother may not do anything at all," Larry said. "She won't like that. She'll find that hard to bear."

"There's that air about the base," Helen said, "of expectancy …"

"We're all waiting," Larry said. "I feel very strongly about this: we're all waiting, even those of us who don't realise we are."

"It's afterwards I worry about," Douglas said, as much to himself as the others. "To reassemble ourselves afterwards – that'll not be easy." Going from rock to rock, sometimes teetering, sometimes falling back, they went to the end of the promontory. Some of the rocks were slippery, and in between there were little pools, with crabs, starfish, barnacles, shells, their surfaces fretted by wind. Now and then they were caught by sea spray, ice-cold, iridescent in the late afternoon sun.

The further out they looked, the brighter it seemed, until it was impossible to tell where the sea ended and the sky began. No-one spoke. It was as if they were held, not by particular features but by the absence of them, the loch drawn out into the sea's immensity like mist into the atmosphere or the earth. There were no small craft about, no dinghies or rowing boats, no yachts.

Months ago, Douglas reflected, he would definitely have been expecting submarines, black shapes emerging into the silence of the loch from the layered silences of its depths as though to give it form and purpose, green and white and blue sea water laving the moulded blacknesses of the bows, the flanks, the conning towers. The surge of the liberated bows had especially held him, the proud towers also, the generous flanks.

Now, however, he could not have said what he was expecting. The sense of expectation was high though. He could not stop himself gazing at the horizon, examining the opposite shore, looking up at the high white clouds tinged now with the pink of evening.

The day before the march Douglas and Larry visited the spot again. This time Edith accompanied them. Conditions were perfect: bright, windless, quite warm. And due to remain so, Douglas reported, punching the air. He was regularly in touch with the Met Office.

In a heavy hat, thick scarf and tartan rug Edith suffered herself to be pushed along the coast road by Larry. Several times he leant forwards, as if to share a joke or confidence with her. If she did not respond, and if Douglas, walking alongside, now and then had to reach out a hand to steady the wheelchair, it did not appear to discourage him. His mood was exultant, impervious.

He was outrunning the occasion, Douglas thought, as well as himself. An excess of zeal. Edith seemed to think so too, her swollen hands held tight into her midriff as if it was there today she was feeling pain, there especially. Her face was white and she was squinting into the sun, mouthing something.

After a bit Douglas noticed that now and then, grimacing and trying to twist, Edith made as if to rise in the wheelchair. He had never seen her do it before. If he hadn't known better, he would have thought she was trying to escape. So single-mindedly did she do it, in such a consumed way, he thought better of asking could he help, was there anything wrong. He simply let his hand rest on the arm of the wheel-chair as it was pushed along the rutted verge.

He wondered then if he was abandoning her to her pain. He enquired about it less, he suspected, than he had before. He suspected also that his will to distract her from it had weakened. If her illness had made her less sensitive to others – quite often now he thought it had – it had probably also made others less sensitive to her, her family especially.

It was not a thought he had had before. But as he walked beside her, trying to come between her and their son's dreadful excitement, he thought it strongly. He had let her go. He had let her go.

"I know we're out here this afternoon to see where the raft's to be launched from," Edith said suddenly. "I know that. And I'd like to say that I admire the spot Larry's chosen. My spirit is there already. I know too that we're going to have a drink in town – a kind of bon voyage it seems, doesn't it? But before that we absolutely must find a place from which tomorrow I can see the march and, most important of all, the raft and the – explosion. I must be high up, very high, looking down. I will be a hawk, an eagle."

What stopped her talking, it appeared, was a fear that she was becoming shrill and dictatorial, a little hysterical even. She made a little gesture of apology.

It had been explained to her that Larry and a friend would be working together, the friend giving a signal, Larry launch-ing the raft. It was what they had thought best, all things considered. Then they would join the march, for purposes of camouflage, and go to the town square for the speeches.

She had received it quietly, almost a joyful quietness, Douglas thought, as if, having foreseen all the options and weighed their virtues, she could rejoice in whichever was chosen. In such moods of equanimity she discounted almost nothing.

It was imperative that they join the march, Douglas thought. Larry especially might otherwise be spotted. Jumping on the promontory, dancing among the trees, darting about on the road: he could imagine it easily. They could join it quietly a few hundred yards down the road and claim, if need be, that they had been on it from the start.

Larry liked the irony of it, marching after all, listening to the speeches, applauding. He said he wouldn't give a damn who he marched with or how many speeches he had to listen to if over the Holy Loch and the American base a huge black mushroom cloud expanded slowly, like a question mark.

"I absolutely must have a clear view of this spot," Edith said again. "Nothing must be in the way, not the march, not the beech trees, not anything."

"Don't worry," Douglas replied. "There are several vantage points. You can take your pick."

He thought of towers and the tops of hills, some of them real, some imaginary. He pictured Edith alone on them in her wheelchair, a rug about her, waiting. While he marched and Larry and Helen managed the raft, the explosion, she would have to be on her own. At least two hours probably. A long time under the circumstances. He would prepare a good picnic for her however, with a thermos of tea. A little tray could be attached to the wheelchair: he would see to it. The tea would help her combat the chill as it grew upon her, as it surely would. Of course he would see to it that she was in a sheltered spot – the edge of a wood, cradled by a hill, under a tree of many branches. Nature had its good places as well as its bad. One of the former would be her companion during the critical hours of the march. He could think of no other companion: in their later years, it seemed, they had drifted from the main, become isolated, with few friends.

"What have you in mind exactly?" Edith asked, making again as if to rise in the wheelchair.

"We can fix you up with some binoculars," Douglas said, borrowing some of Larry's jauntiness. "For a start we can do that. Then there's that place at the top of the road where the three pine trees are. With binoculars you can have a peaceful, uninterrupted view."

"It's not going to be birdwatching, you know!" Edith said scornfully. "I'm going to be watching my son trying to bring off something difficult and dangerous. I'm going to be willing him in spirit to bring the country to its senses. No less! No less!"

"I appreciate that, dear," Douglas said. "How about this then? I've still got that small video camera at home. The explosion could be filmed. You could be in charge. We could sell it to the newspapers, television …"

"What makes you think I could hold them, the binoculars, the camera? For Christ's sake, Douglas!"

"They'll be attached. All you'll need to do …"

"The pain!" Edith cried. "The pain!"

She held up her hands as far as she could, which was not very far, and began to curse. She coughed, as though it was hard for her to get her words out too, coughed and cursed until she was winded, gasping.

Suddenly, Larry stopped the wheelchair and fell to his knees on the grass verge with a little cry. At first it wasn't clear what had possessed him. But then, swivelling on his knees, he reached out to embrace his mother. Soon his head was on her breast and the wheelchair was rocking to his sobs.

To receive him, Edith had to lift her head, which made it seem as if she was staring at the sky, head angled in the interests of precision. Douglas was trembling, and for some reason rubbing his hands. He might have been imploring them not to become too upset or to keep a place for him in whatever was developing.

The next Douglas knew he was grasping the arms of the wheelchair from the front, stooped and bent there as if protecting his family from the skies or struggling to keep the wheelchair from running off the grass verge onto the shore. Then he realised that someone was holding his left hand, someone else his right. The sobs and cries of mother and son were almost indistinguishable. What's more, he seemed to be adding to them, his voice wracked, barely recognisable, issuing from terrible depths.

No sooner had he got himself upright than he was stooping again to touch Larry on the shoulders. He should try to release him from his distress, he felt, this grieving communion with his mother which might have no end. Edith seemed to be attempting it too actually, her gloved hands, high on her son's back, patting it with immense patience and forbearance.

Eventually Larry disengaged himself. He looked ashamed and amazed and as though he wasn't quite sure any more where he was or why he was there. He stumbled unhappily beside the wheelchair while Douglas pushed it, pushed it in the most measured way imaginable, as if all that stood between his family and utter collapse were such movements as these, dogged, careful, faithful, deft, enduring.

They drove to the hilltop from which, more than from any other, Douglas imagined Edith witnessing the explosion, filming it. There was a copse of high trees, round which the road made a U bend, and there were often crows.

For some moments they didn't leave the car but sat very still, trying to settle themselves.

The American base was clearly visible, the path the raft would take across the water easily imaginable. Douglas' thoughts were simple. He believed that the weather would continue fair and that the raft would proceed faultlessly across the windless loch, exploding where planned and very loudly. As though overseen by providence, there would be a clear sequence then: uproar on the base, commands vying with hysteria, piercing whistles, boats launched, but, on shore, the march being resumed after its memorable interruption, Larry, Helen and himself all part of it now, enjoying solidarity, singing perhaps, moving towards the square and the speeches. And Edith on this high hill of course, scarfed against the wind and screaming out with laughter and pride.

"We should perhaps get out and see where you're going to be sitting tomorrow," Douglas said.

His wife and son made no move, seemed greatly to be in need of guidance. It alarmed him. He would have to get them ready for the next day and he wondered how. He wondered if he had the strength, the inspiration.

With immense care, having positioned the wheelchair by the passenger door, he moved Edith's helpless legs and torso out from the car. Larry, who would normally have helped, did nothing. Douglas had the thought that although he had done it thousands of times before, this was like the first. Or like the first time he had done it properly. Perfectly. Proof of his sincerity at last, his love.

"You'll have these extras tomorrow," he said. "Remember that."

"You don't seem to be thinking straight any more, Douglas. I know we're all excited, but how can I possibly …"

"At least give me credit for ingenuity. I've fixed up supports which can be attached to the arms. They'll hold the binoculars here, the camera here."

He demonstrated where they would be and was surprised to feel pride. If you could feel pride in spite of the reactions of others, he thought, there would be less loneliness.

"It's true, mother," Larry said sorrowfully. "He's fixed it for you. There'll be no strain."

"Thank you," Edith said, eyes darting from side to side. "I appreciate it. I appreciate it very much."

Moved himself now, Douglas lifted a hand to hush her. He hadn't known them so formal with each other, so simple.

"It's the least I could do."

"The view is perfect," Edith said. "Just perfect."

It was too. The near shore and even the far shore were clearly visible, the loch and its grey water, the shifting currents even, blue grey under grey, the American base with its harsh lights on already and its winking antennae, its great smoky bulk. A bright evening sky overarched it all, seeming to bestow an immense silence.

Edith had gone very quiet. Douglas had to ask three times how the spot really struck her, and, when at last she responded, she seemed not quite to have understood the question. It was as though she was venturing on meditation and didn't want to be disturbed.

"As I say," she muttered remotely, "it's just perfect."

Larry was the first to spot them, black shapes ahead of their noise, shadows flickering over the hills and the loch. He pointed and ducked but before he could shout the hilltop was blasted by their roar. They flew downwards to the loch, then upwards over the hills on the other side, some banking to the left, some to the right, a manoeuvre they had all seen many times but still, in its symmetrical violation of space and silence, shocking and spectacular.

Minutes after they had gone, Edith stirred, emerging from her silence as if something had occurred to her that should have occurred to her long ago.

"You've no idea how much I'd like a drink. The jets can go to hell, can't they? In spite of all, there seems so much to celebrate. Doesn't there? If you stop to think of it, we're close to being blessed. Or this spot is and we're beneficiaries. D'you know what it reminds me of? I bet you can't guess. It reminds me of that time in Arran when Larry was a baby. We were high up on the hillside that leads to Goat Fell, by the White Water. I was agile then, of course, and in all the future I didn't dream of such shadows as these. You'll not remember it, Larry, but you will, my love, I'm sure."

Touched by her simplicity and directness, Douglas said that he did remember it, although he didn't, he had to be honest. He had thought so much about the times before her illness – almost as though trying to discern the seeds of it – that he had difficulty now in distinguishing one time from another. Like a sunlit plain in the far distance, they stretched north and south, east and west, as far as the eye could see.

Edith's Journal – 6

From the top of Strangeway's Hill – why is it called that? – I had the most wonderful view. It'll be the same tomorrow, the weather forecast assures us.

Now we're on the eve of the march, I'm having these visitations from the past. I still can't see beyond tomorrow – it's just a blank, a darkness – and maybe that's why the past is claiming me so. I can't go forwards, into the future, so I'm vulnerable to the past. At my age, it seems limitless. I didn't know I had so many good memories. Times are coming back to me which I wouldn't have thought were so dear. I've been lucky, I think. Lucky in spite of all.

It's a kind of harvest, you might say, I'm bringing in. Memories falling over one another to get my attention. Like children at a party. I doubt I'll have time for them all, and since I've more time than most, confined to this chair and almost useless now, that shows how many there are. A myriad. I don't feel any strain though. In fact I've never known such an absence of strain. The memories just come, perfect down to the last detail, and in the most revealing sequence imaginable. Randomness doesn't come into it. It's like the story of my life or of parts of it. But it's not as if I'm just living it over again; it's as if I'm doing so with a sense of what it's amounted to. That was never there at the time – oh no I couldn't begin to say what this meaning is. It's simply there in the memories, reassuringly manifest, like a light shining through them, a kind of frame.

I allow myself the fancy that they are a balm to my pain, the memories, that if they were to stop I'd be overcome by pain entirely. What a strange way of regarding myself – as a stage on which either the past lives again or pain dominates, mocks, degrades: I don't like to think I've no say in the matter but it really does seem that way. I've invited neither the memories nor the pain, but here they are, fighting for possession of me. Maybe it's what happens with ruined bodies, overtaxed wills: a time comes when benign and malign forces choose you for their eternal struggle.

I know it's because of the resemblance to what's going to happen tomorrow that I was so struck by it, but let me share one memory.

Larry, aged about seven, is walking before us along a rocky shore. His right hand is raised, purposeful, holding thirty yards or so of string at the end of which, bobbing on small waves, is a toy yacht. We seem to have been walking like this for some time. There's a feeling of great delight but not of safety. Indeed something close to chaos seems to threaten. Larry can only believe that what he's doing has rare delight by constantly turning to look at us and we can only believe it by attending to his every movement. Were he to look round and find us looking away or were we actually to do this, the whole scene would fracture. The yacht would bob away, a storm would get up, someone might drown. It doesn't happen though for it's one of those days when everyone's timing is perfect. We walk on and on, right round the bay to the lighthouse where Larry reins in his yacht.

It was a bay in the north of Arran. Beyond it is the Irish Sea. It wouldn't profit me to return though. Only the naive believe in returns, revisits. In my experience, landscape never delivers the goods on occasions like that. The very reverse: it stands still as the grave, making you feel you've made a fool of yourself. Which you have. Its neutrality is what you notice; it's not partial, doesn't give a damn for our nostalgia. We err by not understanding this.

The closer we get to the march, the more the memories come. Hour by hour. Such a quickening. Will they stop so that tomorrow I can concentrate on Larry? Will there prove to be a providence or is it quite random what'll happen? Certainly, when dear Douglas parked me at the top of the hill today, I had the most profound sense of being providentially buoyed up. In agony half an hour before (I'd never tell him, but Larry's posturing and false optimism didn't help), I felt suddenly wonderfully still and concentrated. Perhaps it's easier for us with useless ravaged bodies to feel we're instruments of higher powers, I don't know, but I did really feel it. Why not, if you stop to think about it? If God can ask Abraham to sacrifice Isaac, why can He not ask things of us, the ill and elderly?

I appear to be able to accept now that all I can do tomorrow is be with Larry in spirit. (The filming is really incidental.) Until recently though I couldn't. I kept thinking there must be something unique for me, Edith Low, to do. Only if the pain becomes terrible am I likely to think it again. When the pain is like that, you see, I'm a different person. The world is not as it is now. I seem to feel that extreme measures are necessary.

It might help if I rehearse what's going to happen tomorrow – firstly, what we hope will happen, secondly, what we dread.

Douglas and Larry will park me at the top of the hill. I'll have food with me and tea. There will be supports for the binoculars and the video camera. I'll train the glasses on Larry in his cove and set the camera going in plenty of time to film the explosion. Larry's given me an approximate time – 3 p.m. I'll start filming before that. After the explosion, which will halt the march for quite some time, I believe, Larry and the friend who is helping him (a retired teacher, I'm told) will join the march. They'll go to the town square and listen to some speeches maybe. Douglas and Larry will then meet up and drive up the hill to collect me.

I'll probably be very cold by then but happy. Happy! There will be celebrations on the hill top.

If it goes wrong, it will probably be because of problems launching the raft. It'll blow up in Larry's face. Or it'll get launched but blow up too soon or too late or not at all. Or it'll all go to plan but Larry or his friend or both will be arrested. If Larry is arrested or injured or worse, Douglas will come and get me immediately he finds out.

They're both very concerned about me, I must say, almost more than they are about themselves and each other actually. They feel for me being on the sidelines.

At least each is doing what he thinks is right. Neither is compromising. Neither am I really.

I don't think I've ever loved them so much. Or felt myself so much loved. I think I could describe myself as happy.

IX

The day of the march dawned bright and still. Early jets had left vapour trails that looked like the ribs of heaven. Great Easter weather. At seven o'clock Larry came into his parents' bedroom to tell them so; smiling broadly, drew back the curtains to demonstrate the truth of his words.

Discovering the sleepers, exacerbating the discomforts of waking, the light seemed cruel, but beautiful then, solicitous.

Edith was especially slow to waken, moaning, making little jerking movements with her arms and legs, as if the drugs had bunched up in her system and were exploding. Larry sat on the side of the bed, his smile still rather deliberate, and, when the moment came, helped her to sit up, fixing pillows behind her as he did so. Her grey hair fell over her face. He drew it back carefully, securing it at the nape of her neck. She muttered thanks but complained she'd had a bad night, that the day could only bring improvement. As if realising only then what that day was, she broke off, her head falling forwards onto her chest.

Larry told them to rest where they were. He had made their breakfasts and would bring them in on trays.

Which he did, first serving his mother, then his father, and then, as if it was someone's birthday or an anniversary, sitting in a chair in the morning sun watching them.

His mother moved her mouth down to her hand, tugging at her toast, his father, who had barely spoken, ate with more formality in bed than he did at table.

"When does the march start?" Douglas asked, although he had asked it the evening before.

"One o'clock," Larry said.

143

"And the raft? How is it? Did it go into the car alright?"

"It's in the boot now. It went in easily. I knew it would."

"Have you been up long?" Edith asked. "You look as if you have."

"Since five-thirty. It's been very still and bright. I've heard birds singing I've never heard before. I even saw a fox, up by the observatory."

"I'll be glad to get going," Edith said. "I didn't have a good night."

"Me too," Larry said. "It's been a long wait. Tonight though, if all goes well, we'll have a party."

"Just the three of us," Douglas said, looking out into the garden where the hut in which Larry had built the raft and the explosive device stood. The wood had weathered, not so white, a little browner now.

"I don't know about a party," Edith said in a reduced voice. "I've never known about them. Shall we wait and see? If we have one, we have one. If not … not."

"Let me help you get ready, dear," Douglas said. "I feel the call of the day."

Larry left the room with the trays. He was smiling again, as if everything that was happening was happening to plan.

In his pyjamas, Douglas knelt by his wife's bed, pulled back the bedclothes and, with the utmost care, moved first her right leg, then her left, then her right again towards the edge of the bed. He could tell that she was in pain; she was trying to act as if her body wasn't really there, as if the physical was an illusion, the most stubborn of all.

The way he bowed his head, it might have been an illusion Douglas regretted being unable to share.

The small engine Larry had attached to the back of the raft had started each time it had been asked to. He had no reason to doubt it, he said. The explosive device hadn't been tested – he couldn't afford a second one – but he had reason to have faith in it also. His main concern was that he hadn't tested the engine on water, merely in the privacy of his hut. He didn't think that being on a raft-like structure travelling over water would make much difference though, particularly since the loch was as still as he had ever seen it, with no waves to lap into the engine and harm it.

"Let me show you," Larry said, opening the boot and lifting off a cover.

The raft was smaller than Douglas remembered, neater, more compact, with a curved bow and a raised stern. The explosive device had been strapped to another raised area, in the middle, two fuses running through plastic tubes to the stern. There were two fuses, Larry explained, because one might be extinguished, though with the plastic tubes this was very unlikely. The fuses were slow burning, and would take four minutes to reach the device. He had programmed the engine so that the raft would be about thirty yards from the base when the explosion took place.

He explained it all in a low voice, now and then gesturing, once looking in the direction of the base. If he had any feelings of regret or apprehension that the period of planning and preparation was over, he didn't show them. He seemed given over rather to a kind of willed triumphalism.

Douglas himself had mixed feelings – anticipations of success, yet regret, anxiety – and thought that Edith would have too. What would it be like afterwards, when they didn't have this day to look forward to? In what state would they pass beyond it? What fruits would it bear? What shadows cast? He leant against the car, listening to Larry, his excited explanations.

"Even if it veers a little left or right, it'll be near enough. But I don't see it veering on a day like this. Have you ever known such calm? Have you ever?"

Douglas began thinking of Helen. They were to meet her later, at the beech trees. He found himself picturing her as she might appear through binoculars – through

Edith's, for instance, if her vantage point was closer. A trim figure in a tightly belted overcoat, legs slightly apart, hands deep in pockets, collar turned up as in expectation of rain or coldness.

Whenever he had thought of her recently, for some reason, he had thought of her like this, as through binoculars, before the beech trees, the loch behind, a high spring sky above, moving as though enthralled or possessed. It was wonderful to picture her so; he couldn't seem to do it otherwise. It was like a fragment from a saga, a fragment by which the saga would eventually be known, illuminated.

No such particularity would be possible for Edith from the hilltop, of course. She would see the long line of the march curving along the coast, she would see the beech trees, the loch, opaque and dazzling, the explosion, the cloud, the mid-afternoon darkness. Again as through binoculars Douglas seemed to see her beholding it all, head in the wheelchair flung back in shock and pain, a dreadful agitation.

"Oh well," he heard himself say, "this is it. Time has got us here as it will surely take us beyond it."

Larry nudged him. Having looked the raft and explosive device over carefully, Edith was trembling, appeared suddenly exhausted.

"Let's get you settled, my dear," Douglas said, moving the wheelchair round to the side of the car. "Are you cold?"

"It's not cold that I feel," she said. "I may be cold but I don't feel it. No, it's not that at all."

She seemed concerned to say more, but didn't. Settled in the passenger seat, she was very still, still in both face and body. Douglas couldn't think of anything to say: anything would have been an interruption. He thought of embracing her, but she was too remote for that also.

In the depths of her immobility then he thought he detected a smile, or not so much a smile as a disposition to smile. He couldn't be sure, but turning to fold up the wheelchair and put it away, he had that feeling: sub-merged, a sort of palimpsest, spirit beneath flesh, there had been a smile.

In the back seat Larry was writing in a notebook, making calculations. Douglas looked over to see what they were, but the notebook was snapped shut, put away. Larry was then almost as silent as his mother.

Mindful of his cargo, Douglas drove very carefully. (He was doing everything very carefully, he realised, as for the first or last time.) Too carefully, Larry suddenly said. At this rate they would be stopped by the police for slow driv-ing. Not even new drivers went this slow. He went a little faster, wondering if he was the only person on the roads today with something to hide. The rear-view mirror was largely filled with Larry's head, wobbling nervously. His son. His son the mastermind.

They approached the hilltop from which Edith was to witness the afternoon's events. It worried Douglas that she hadn't spoken since getting into the car. Normally the motion of the car had the effect of relaxing her a little. Larry was obviously worried too; he was leaning well for-wards, a hand on his mother's arm, stroking it, massaging it, now and then saying something, immediately looking to see if there had been any effect. But neither words nor touch was getting through. Twice she did clear her throat, as though to speak, but didn't, which suddenly made it seem not so much a failure of will as of capacity. She was, for the moment, dumbstruck, literally so.

Douglas put out a hand also, resting it on Edith's thigh, steering very precisely with the other. He couldn't be sure that she felt it though, almost couldn't be sure that she heard. He simply hoped that she did, that she was aware of their concern, their patience and their love, their goodwill.

They settled her in the silence of the hilltop, under the solicitous pines. To one arm of the wheelchair binoculars had been attached by means of a rod, to the other a video camera. Larry trained them on what he called "his patch" of water. All Edith had to do to look through them, he explained, was lean six inches to the left or six inches to the right.

They waited with her for about half an hour, talking quite simply. How there were more cars now than there had been earlier; how bright and clear the day was, how still; how they wished she could be with them, either on the march or helping with the raft, the explosion; how each group would have its own banner – "Dumbarton C.N.D.", "Lochgilphead C.N.D.", "Belfast C.N.D."; how from the stillness of her hilltop she might be able to hear snatches of song, songs of the sixties for the middle-aged, songs of brotherhood and hope and love, songs of threat and defiance from the young, bitter, mordant, jesting.

Larry mentioned he was counting on a certain rowdiness among the marchers to give him cover. Nothing would drown out the sound of the explosion of course. On the contrary. All would be silenced and humbled. All eyes, Edith's especially, would be on the loch, the base. To some it might seem then as if hours passed before the march got under way again. Those at the back would have to wait for word to be passed down the length of the march. How long that would take Larry didn't know, but, people being what they were, the story would be changed as it was told, as it travelled.

Edith alone would be in a position to give a true account. Larry was counting on her. An oral account and the video. She could write it up afterwards. He and Douglas and Helen would be too close to know, too excited, too frightened. He held her hand tightly as he spoke, stroking the top of it, almost as though he was trying to get her to make a vow. She bore it with good patience.

When the time came for them to leave, Edith found her voice, but not the voice they were used to, not low, thickened by pain and medication, slightly rasping. It was cleansed and refreshed, light and quiet, extraordinarily even, issuing as from some imperturbability of childhood. Stooping to embrace her, Douglas wondered if it was to repossess her voice so astonishingly that she had been silent for most of the morning – to repossess it and say what she now proceeded to say.

"Whatever happens today, however it turns out, it's been worthwhile. Your project is a grand one, Larry, and your decision to march is immensely worthy too, Douglas. Don't worry about me. I'll be perfectly safe here, watching with the greatest pride. I have my binoculars and a flask of tea, I have the camera. It's very peaceful here, no distractions of any kind, no ugly sounds, no ugly smells. The only ugliness is the base, but we've come to terms with that, I think, in our different ways. No, up here I'll be just fine. It's like returning to the elements actually. What more could I want? What more?"

She found the strength to embrace her husband and son in turn. Then they were off, Douglas driving slowly and in silence down to the coast road. Now and then he caught a glimpse of Edith in the rear-view mirror. She seemed to be staring out to sea.

It took him only a few moments to reach the beech trees, but in the course of them he realised that spring had come. It caught him by the throat, made him immediately walk away from the car after he had got out of it, leaving Larry to greet Helen, lead her to the car and show her the raft.

Held by what seemed the authority of spring, he came close to regarding them as a pair of cranks, welcoming each other with comical eagerness, too many grins, too many gestures. Of course, he must seem odd to them too – disengaged, irresolute, a little foolish. He didn't mind: for the moment his question to himself was whether it mightn't be possible one day to make a life of such disengagement – beyond the dialectic and rhetoric of protest and opposition to live evenly and sweetly. As though in thrall to spring and his wife's parting words – to her temper on the hilltop above all perhaps – he considered it, was still doing so when Helen sought him out among the trees.

"How are you then?" she asked. "Palely loitering? There's the raft to help carry."

"I know, Helen. I know."

She looked at him impatiently. He smiled in a way he knew would irritate her, indulgently, as if she was not quite making sense. She turned and walked briskly away. He didn't like the briskness; it seemed out of place.

He couldn't see what made the raft so heavy. It may have looked like a big toy but it didn't feel like one. It sobered him, carrying it through the trees to where Larry had decided it should lie, hidden by branches, until it was time for it to be taken further, to the bush on the promontory.

He drove the car a little way up the hill then, parking it in a line of cars – early marchers, he assumed – and went back to the beech trees.

Larry and Helen were gazing out across the loch, as carefully hidden by the trees, Larry was claiming, as the raft was by branches. There was no need to worry, he said: it was a friendly copse, one of the earth's good places. It would not allow any harm to come to them. Helen said nothing, whether agreeing with him or humouring him, Douglas could not tell.

The loch was as glass, the light off it glittering, blinding. They could hear traffic on the other side, cars, buses and motor-bikes going to the various assembly points, their sounds as clear to the ear as the trees and clouds reflected in the loch were to the eye. From the base came the usual noises, purged just a little of their usual unpleasantness, Douglas fancied, by the day's stillness. Voices could be heard, accents distinguished: Bronx, Texan, Deep South. And sometimes there was laughter, echoing around them in the trees and so detached from its causes as to sound crazy.

"Listen to them!" Helen was sitting with her arms hugging her knees, her knees drawn up to her chin. "D'you think they'll even notice the march?"

"Who knows? They're certainly very used to them. But that's all to the good: it'll make their shock all the greater."

"It will, you're right." She turned to him. "You've thought it all out, haven't you?"

He shrugged his shoulders, as if it wasn't the time for compliments.

Douglas had nothing to say. Now that they had hidden the raft, he could attend once more to the spring. He couldn't think of a better place; here if nowhere else the seasons would run true. Yet it was the place chosen by the Americans for their base, by Larry for his demonstration. Such interlocking worlds: for the moment, it seemed, he couldn't take it. These offences at first hand, how they troubled the heart.

Edith had said she was returning to the elements. Something like that. Did he understand what she meant? See the possibility of it? He thought he did, and wondered a little about the march, the sense of it. On the very verge of it to lose resolve though. Possibly he didn't believe in anything very much. That might be it. Uninspired, he circled the inspired to see where they pointed.

Perhaps then he should have stayed with Edith? She had seemed closer to wisdom today than he or Larry or Helen. Up there on her hill she had struck a rich vein somehow. She would be hearing the birds and noticing the light, the windless clarity. She would be readying herself. The eloquence of her recovered voice.

Of course, a cripple, she had no option. Did that mean her disease was her salvation? How could that be? He imagined her, able-bodied, sitting with Larry as Helen was

151

now, talking in low tones, proudly conspiratorial, looking forward to the explosion, possible martyrdom.

He found that he was holding himself tightly, rocking a little in the dappled shade, and thought, "No wonder!"

And Larry. Probably he felt only contempt for his father today. Douglas looked to see if it was so, but there were no signs. All he noticed was that in profile he resembled his mother, some compactness about the mouth, bold, ruminative. Why hadn't he noticed it before? Would he have spotted it the other way round, searching Edith for signs of impatience, contempt?

It was Saturday, April 13th. There was a Sabbath softness to things however. He wondered at his dreaminess, the march and explosion so close. It was like a last turn in the ways of idleness.

Turning to his companions, he found that they had moved further away. Helen was telling Larry about her husband. What struck Douglas was the care with which she was selecting the details. He had heard them all before, but never in this order, with this highlighting. Of course, who you told your story to affected how you told it; affected what you thought it was; affected who you thought you were even, telling it.

Her tone was earnest, excited. It was as if, Douglas thought, she was trying to account for how, married for so long to a man like Barnie, she had come to be here on the Holy Loch doing dangerous business with a young man she hardly knew, his father her lover perched on the sidelines.

"When I married Barnie, he seemed older than me. After five years of marriage, though, he seemed to have got younger, or I older, I was never clear which. Towards the end, then, he got much older again: decades seemed to separate us. When he died, it was of old age. Death just came to get him. He'd never had much initiative: it was I who supplied it. He didn't mind, though. Being bossed about was what kept him going – he admitted it! Another man might have resented it – your father, for instance – but not Barnie."

"What was the age difference?" Larry asked.

"Twenty-two years."

"My lifetime roughly."

There was a pause. Helen looked over her shoulder and made as if to smile – most oddly, as though she was offering goodwill to Douglas in case he should be in need of it. He didn't think he was, however. The smile seemed forced, merely dutiful, and he thought she turned away from him more easily than she had turned towards him. Quickly she resumed her talk about Barnie, the day of his death, the manner of it, the kindliness of undertakers, the unsatisfactoriness of cremation, the enigma of dust and ashes.

Larry didn't seem to be listening any more, however, or seemed to be listening to something quite beyond Helen's words. It made her seem gauche, Douglas thought, guilty of a kind of silliness. He would have reached out a hand to her had she not been fifteen yards away, sitting next to his son.

"The march," Larry said. "I think I hear it. Listen!"

To begin with, Douglas couldn't hear anything. Ears not what they were. He sat with his head cocked, thinking, "I wasn't there at the start. I'll join it later." Maybe he had been mistaken about the starting time. No matter. Time today was as long as the coast road, with as many pockets, as many pools. You spun your own time within it. There was room for most.

Not so much entering the silence, then, as emerging from it, spun from it, a sound as of distant waterfalls. Quite a light sound at first but becoming heavier, graver, more measured. Then, as out of silence the sound of treading, marching, had come, so now out of that voices arose, a kind of subdued hubbub accompanying movement, fitful though, fitful in spite of the stillness.

For a moment Douglas felt strange, as though troubled by the fancy that the march was coming as much out of the past as from the west, where the loch began.

Larry and Helen were listening intently. They might have been at prayer, so bowed their heads and motionless. It wouldn't have surprised Douglas to find that they were holding hands. He didn't look; their endeavour was not his, their energies not his either.

The longer they sat in the copse, the stiller it became, confusingly so, a stillness within the overall stillness, as it were, a sort of rival stillness.

Some time later – how much, Douglas couldn't have said – they became aware that the earth beneath them was trembling. The march was approaching. Shouts could be heard, a sort of drumming too, reverberation at once heard and felt.

Larry was on his feet, peering through the trees, hands spread for silence. Helen remained where she was, legs drawn up, chin on her knees. Soon Douglas was on his feet also, straining to see what Larry was seeing.

Banners and emblems, dominating patches of red and white and yellow and blue, were approaching up the road as though it was they who were bringing the marchers rather than the other way round. When the head of the march drew level with the copse, there seemed for an instant to be a profound silence, as of something seen suddenly in dumb show. Then noise burst out again, shouts and snatches of song above the tramping of feet, laughter, cries.

What struck Douglas most as the march went by – beside the fact that he was not yet on it – was its variety, groups, phalanxes, contingents of all kinds, some murmurous, some raucous, some singing, some appearing to have embraced silence. So relentlessly did it come on, streaming past as they sheltered in the copse, that Douglas wondered if Larry had been wrong in thinking there would be gaps between the groups, during one of which he would launch his raft.

"There are always more people at the head of a march than in the middle or at the back. It's always denser here. Terribly dense sometimes, dangerously so. It thins out the further back you go. You come upon gaps then – like firebreaks really. They save the contingents for one another; they give definition. All we have to do is wait for these to appear. Yes. Another law of marches is that the further back you go, the bigger the firebreaks are. Not that I'll be waiting too long. What would be the point of having my explosion when most of the march is past? Talk about performing to an empty house!"

Unseen among the trees, they watched as a contingent from Dundee went by, then one from Bradford, then one from Inverness. Then there was a large one from Aberdeen, seeming to sway as it went, its yellow banners swaying too.

Larry was right. The gaps between the groups were getting larger, though the numbers in the groups were about the same. Their time was approaching, the time for the well ordered afternoon to be stopped in its tracks. Larry looked from Helen to Douglas and back again. Then he put an arm round his father, his grin as he surveyed the march at once edgy and proprietorial. This was his audience and he would command it.

The gesture should have been his, Douglas thought. He couldn't think of anything to say even. Neither to Larry nor Helen. Not a word. If it was not fear exactly, it was some kind of sympathetic trepidation on his son's behalf that bore most of the marks of it. He forced himself to smile, held the smile in the hope of encouraging his companions.

Larry said it was time to carry the raft to its launching place, checking his watch as he said it, as if everything today had been planned to the last second and he, Larry, had planned it.

This time they bore it solemnly, with an air almost of ritual, Helen going in front to clear the way. By the bush on the promontory they lowered it to the water, holding it there for a moment, feeling the water accept it, buoy it up. Larry knelt, smiling, checking it, Douglas and Helen looking on, looking for a sign that all was well. All seemed to be, for Larry stood up and looked proudly across the water.

When Helen slipped her arm through his, Douglas closed his eyes. He would not be marching now. Next year perhaps but not this. It had been decided. Necessities closer to hand had got the better of him. The heroic ingenuity of his son's project.

He didn't feel defeated though, weak and in thrall to other wills. His sense was of a gracious welcome rather from these companions who had stepped into the shadows before him.

He was sorry Edith didn't know. Probably she did though, having foreseen it. A good wife foresaw much, what came from the good in you as well as what came from the bad.

"Anytime you're ready," Larry said quietly. "No-one out there has a clue what's going to happen. You realise that?"

For a moment it seemed a tremendous advantage, the secrecy of it, they, not the Americans, commanding the loch, the future. Douglas felt suddenly very proud, not just of Larry, author of the spectacular defiance, but of Helen also and even himself, late convert though he was. And of his wife, Edith, superbly watchful on her high hill, intensely proud of herself yet by now surely very agitated and alone.

"Good luck," he said, at once darkened and quickened by the image of Edith. "Good luck!"

"I appreciate it very much," Larry said simply, "your staying on here to help. All our energies are going in the one direction now. We can't fail."

"Good luck, Larry," Helen said, touching his arm.

"I'll meet the two of you afterwards, in the march

somewhere. Yes, somewhere along the road in the march we'll meet again. See you."

He stooped again to the raft, which was bobbing slightly on the water. His hands as he touched and steadied it were slow and affectionate. He might have been discovering it for the first time.

"It's like one of his childhood projects," Douglas said as they made their way over the rocks to the copse. "A childhood project that's entered adulthood. It's as if all those early years were just preparation. You never think it at the time; you think it's just childhood, dreams, play."

He was pleased as he spoke, however, smiling.

"It throws a long shadow," Helen said, "childhood."

Dust had been raised by the march so that some walked with hands to their eyes and some were coughing. "Mothers Against The Bomb" was passing, but there were fathers too, a few with children on their shoulders. One in a kilt was playing a mouth organ with one hand and doing a little jig, creating a space about him as he did so, guarding the space jealously, gesturing others away from it. Two little boys were imitating him, vying with each other, close to mockery. Then in a wheelchair came a little girl with a hump, the hump higher and bigger than her head, which was lolling to one side. The man pushing her was very tall and bore himself proudly, seeming to stare over the heads of the marchers to some distant kingdom. Douglas wondered how many marches the girl had been on, whether she had any freedom at all. Borne forwards through dust and noise under banners towards sunset. What contact with others? Little. None. A sightless traveller.

"Mothers Against The Bomb" seemed to mark the end of one stage of the march. Over a hundred yards away they could see another approaching, creeping over the rim of a low hill.

They emerged quietly from the trees and went down the road to their positions, Helen at the first corner, Douglas at the second, exactly as in their rehearsal.

157

They might have been rehearsing it once a day for a year, Douglas felt, so lightly and gladly did he move, so clearly see. It was the same for Helen, he was sure, going – as he seemed to be – quite soundlessly to her position, as though woven into the world somehow, into the spring sunshine, the great stillness over loch and hills, the road, even, the contours of the land.

They held their positions with an air of noble patience, Douglas looking behind him, in the direction of the march, Helen looking at Douglas, very intently.

When the head of the march dipped out of sight for a moment, Douglas dropped his arm, Helen hers too. Running forwards, he saw Larry emerge from a crouching position – try to rather, for it seemed for an instant that his son was moving heavily, as if the long wait had confused him. He recovered quickly, though, was soon crouched again, a few yards away, where the bush was.

The sound that broke the silence then didn't seem to Douglas to augur well. Too loud. Much too loud. A high-powered lawnmower or a chainsaw. He hadn't imagined the raft's engine would sound like this; he had thought of something gentler. It was surely a miscalculation. It wouldn't do.

He grabbed Helen's hand and ran with her back to the copse, a particular spot there from which he had calculated that, unseen from the road, they would be able to watch whatever happened.

In the copse the roar of the engine seemed to have got caught up with the echoes, creating and destroying them alternately. Blue smoke was drifting among the trees, and there was a smell of petrol.

Larry had said that he would join them on the march afterwards, but here he was, dodging through the trees, grinning, pointing.

"Perfect speed! Straight as an arrow! Look!"

When Douglas caught sight of the raft, however, it

wasn't like this at all. It didn't appear to be going in a straight line and its speed didn't appear to be regular. It was moving in a wide arc, first towards the middle of the loch, then, faltering slightly, towards the base. It was also bouncing a little, from side to side and from back to front, making a screaming noise now rather than a roar.

Douglas' hope was that it would explode before it sank, before his son was humiliated, before he heard him boast again that all was well. All his enthusiasms, he realised, had at some point bordered on the crazy.

"Marvellous!" he heard him declare.

When it came, about fifty yards from the base, the explosion was terrific. At first a crack, then a boom, then a roar which became roaring. Terrific too were the violent echoes which were thrown back immediately from the surrounding hills. An extraordinary outpouring of dense black smoke, then, convulsively spinning and rolling its way across the water and upwards. The mushroom cloud over which Larry had been brooding for months, however, had not appeared. Suddenly, though, like features out of darkness, a face upon the waters, it manifested itself, holding its shape remarkably as the convulsions of smoke and fire continued underneath – seemed to be feeding it actually, helping it to a kind of perfection.

In full dignity then it was before them, entirely itself over the barely visible base from which now came cries of alarm and distress.

As if it was a shape as natural as any under the sun. The most violent of reactions creating stillness. Stillness at the heart of chaos.

At last the echoes ceased, leaving panic and uproar on the base and along the coast.

Douglas found that he had gripped Helen with one hand, Larry with the other. To support or be supported, he did not know. Larry was laughing, Helen silent. The copse was rocking and cracking and the light was strange. He

159

was reaching for words, it seemed, unsure which awed him the more, the violence of the explosion or Larry's stage-managing of it. Ardent congratulations seemed in order, but when he spoke it was in fear, his voice raised against the wail of sirens, against clamour.

"We'd better get into the march as quickly as possible," he said. "Anyone caught outside is bound to be questioned."

"Let them question us!" Larry laughed. "We've nothing to hide, less to fear. They can't touch us!"

"You smell of smoke and fire," Helen said, "and I don't think you're making sense."

"Oh I'm making sense all right!" Larry replied angrily.

"Come on, for Christ's sake!" Douglas said.

He urged them, the one silent, the other cackling, out of the copse and into a field of tall grasses. There, bent double, they went towards the town. The shadow of a hedge was on the grasses and the light under the mushroom cloud was murky. Moving through the grasses was difficult, like being in a dark green sea with unconscionable currents. Larry was shouting and cackling still, indiscriminate curses and praises, it seemed, as if the mounting clamour had freed him from all prudence and decorum.

"That's done for them! Bloody Yanks, stuffed at last! Ever met a Yank, Helen? Forget it. Stick to me and your man here! Now you're talking! Quality is quality! Mother too! Here's to mother! Mother!"

Coughing stopped him, seeds from the grasses most probably, for which Douglas was thankful, for otherwise he would have had to do it himself, he or Helen or both, standing up in the grasses, to tell him to shut up, waist deep, shouting.

The ground was heavy but it was not so much this and the thick grasses that stopped them as the realisation that they had drawn level with a large contingent. Its red banners could be seen over the hedge, some moving jerkily, some stationary. Fugitives, supporting each other again, they huddled under the hedge. They could clearly hear voices, men's mainly, a mood of consternation and alarm, though with the odd, high burst of laughter.

Some thought a submarine had blown up and that they would be done for soon themselves. Some that it was an accident on the base, not as serious as it seemed. Some an attack by Russia. Some a plane crash, out of the blue and into the Holy Loch. Some a terrorist attack, someone an earthquake. A woman with a sing-song voice said it would be like this with the real thing: they would be away from their homes and families, there would be this kind of premature dusk …

The cloud had strayed to the west a little, still expanding, losing its shape only at the top. Just from considering it, Douglas thought, you couldn't tell what had caused it. Many would be looking up. All probably. Eyes to heaven. It would give them a chance to slip through the hedge, be marching before anyone noticed them.

Eventually the contingent got under way again, in thrall to the cloud but defiant, making a lot of noise. When it was almost past, Douglas helped his companions through a gap in the hedge, hoping to find some stragglers they could join and finding them, the elderly mostly, walking as though speculatively, eyes raised to the cloud which, as it slid westwards, was beginning to flatten.

They were tired now, Douglas saw, very tired, barely responsible for their movements, weak and wandering ones. Even here though he made as if to guide them, as if he alone was walking well and strongly. Neither were the stragglers walking well, he noticed, in this grainy light of premature dusk with the road going slightly uphill.

Putting his arms through theirs, he walked with Larry and Helen down the centre of the road. It got even darker. There was excited birdsong, gatherings of birds in the hedges and bushes.

Not to be overtaken by the contingent behind, Douglas increased the pace a little. He could hear it approaching, could feel it in the road even, young feet, vigorous feet, keen to be part of the action, history's extras.

"All we need to do is keep going," Douglas said. "Eventually we'll reach the town and eventually there will be speeches."

"Speeches, speeches," Larry muttered.

"What's wrong with speeches?" Helen asked.

"Suit yourself," Larry said.

Larry's confused gait on the one hand, Helen's weakening one on the other, Douglas pressed on, round a corner, through the damaged light. A breeze had got up, moving the cloud further to the west and threatening its dispersal. It also brought what had escaped them so far, the smell of the explosion, a most unpleasant one, mean, acrid, gritty. Something irritated their eyes and caught at their throats.

"Sorry about this," Larry said proudly. "I hadn't anticipated a smell. Really I hadn't."

Douglas could tell, from little feelings of irritation – at the contingent in front for going too slowly, at the one behind for seeming to bear down on them, at Larry for acting as if, the explosion accomplished, there was now nothing left to say or do – that he was worrying about Edith. He had been away from her for over two hours. How had she been when the explosion took place, as the cloud formed and later passed over her? How did you cope with such excitement if you couldn't move, were probably in pain, had no-one to share it with? She would have wet or fouled herself, he feared, as she had done a few times before, when badly overwrought.

Saying that she wanted to find out what other marchers were thinking, Helen left them for a while.

Larry had no such concerns. He was stumbling along beside his father as if he was being led, taken to a point from which the next stage of his life would be explained to him. Whether he wanted such an explanation was unclear. The hell of anti-climax, Edith might have said. That was her state too perhaps, wet and fouled up there on the hilltop, abandoned by the gods of energy and design. They should make haste to go to her, Douglas thought. They should skip the speeches. Why had he ever thought he would stay for them?

"How are you?" Douglas asked.

"Strange. They're like the days of wrath."

"They surely look like them. You've done well."

"I'd like to drink a toast to mother."

"We should go to her."

"Yes."

"As soon as we can. You first; you'll be quicker."

"Helen? Will she come too?" Larry grinned sideways.

"What do you think?" Douglas answered coldly.

"We could say we met her on the march, under the cloud, that she was hysterical and that we offered her comfort."

"What have you made of it all?" Douglas asked after a pause. "How do you rate it?"

"Too soon to say," Larry answered. "For a moment back there I feared it had been pointless, schoolboyish, not much more than a prank."

"And now?"

"I like the darkness. That's a bonus."

Head rolling, hands fluttering like wounded birds, Larry was wandering all over the road. Even to his father he didn't seem all there. If they wanted to arrest someone on suspicion of terrorism, Douglas thought, they could do worse than to start here.

"She's very thorough, isn't she?" Larry suddenly said. "Helen, I mean. Doesn't leave a stone unturned. Such a passion for detail. Providential. I couldn't have done without her today. Nor could you, I suspect. Where is she anyway?"

"Here she is."

Ducking under drifting smoke and looking pleased with herself, Helen was coming briskly back to them.

"Larry!" she called, reaching out to him in one of his wanderings. "Come here! Listen!"

They heard again that some thought there had been a nuclear explosion and that what they were doing was wandering in a doomed twilight. Others were of the opinion that it was an attempt by the Americans to scare off the marchers, others a World War Two mine blowing up, others an I.R.A. initiative. Most however didn't know but wanted to find out.

"You've certainly got them thinking, very agitated. Running scared, actually. I sense a lot of panic."

"Panic? I don't see much of that."

"Up there there is. Don't you doubt it."

Larry looked uncertain. It was as if Helen's words could be taken in two ways, either as confirming the great success of his venture or as hinting at some vainglory at its heart.

They were entering the town now, the march slowing, held up in the small squares and narrow streets, directed here and there by the police. After the open countryside, it was also noisier, raucous congestion, restlessness. The townspeople, making their own noise, had lined the streets to watch. The makings of a rabble, Douglas thought. The town seemed too small, not just for the marchers but for the rumours they had brought. (Like flames of different colours, the rumours tried now this street, now that, now this structure, now that, until everything had been licked, unsettled.)

He saw that Larry was looking for an opportunity to dodge away up one of the side streets to the hilltop. His face was suddenly grave and calm, as in remembrance of the hilltop, its stillness. For quite some time now Edith would have been up there surveying the afternoon, filming it, Douglas hoped, for the media, posterity. On his own face too, he imagined, there would be such a look, hope and gravity in equal measures.

"See you," Larry said, dodging off.

"Edith," Douglas said in response to Helen's enquiring look.

"She'll be alright," she said. "Cold and stiff but alright. Triumphant probably. Don't worry."

"Cold certainly," Douglas said. "I'll join them in a minute. Push her down to the car. Or bring the car up to her. Whichever."

The climb from here would be steep, but if he were to take it steadily, shoulders back and breathing well, he would make it in good time and with energy to spare if Edith was in a bad way. She would have wet and fouled herself, he was sure. The great worry over Larry. The medication. The wheelchair cramps. Loneliness. It couldn't be otherwise. They would have to get her home as quickly as possible. He would clean her then as kindly and temperately as he could, talking about the explosion, the triumph, to distract her. The worst of his tasks. The worst for both of them. His spirit was insufficient. Or had been, until now.

Quite quickly however Larry was back. He said that Edith was not there. Gone. He had looked for her briefly round about, but in vain. He had shouted her name, hands cupped to his mouth (of this he gave a quick, distracted demonstration). Then he gestured fretfully, as if the hilltop was a spirit as well as a place, responsible somehow for his mother's disappearance.

All three set off up the hill, leaning into a breeze, leaving the clamour of the crowds gradually behind and below them.

Douglas had to admit he wasn't surprised. Had he really expected her to be still there? To remain in the one spot for hours? Unmoving, a mere spectator? As though asleep in the sun or before television?

Asking the question like this, he realised that he hadn't expected it. Apart from anything else, she could cover considerable distances in the wheelchair, or had once been able to do so. And she wasn't afraid of risks.

Struggling up the hill, though, always just ahead of Larry and Helen, he couldn't imagine what risks she might have taken today. Merely knew that she would have taken one. Suddenly realised also that, all things considered, it would have been much more surprising had she still been there, waiting for them obediently on the hilltop, than not. How foolish not to guess at these further reaches in others, their main track, for all one knew. Climbing fast, he cursed himself.

"I think we should try this one," Larry said, gasping, perspiring, "I didn't check it."

Douglas felt it might have been because the road was very narrow, with large houses set well back from the road, inhospitably self-contained, that they ran down it as they did. It was as if they had no business being there and should pass through as quickly as possible. Three people unused to running, running abreast, labouring, gasping unashamedly, keys and loose change jingling.

They were running in utter panic, Douglas then saw, but whether the panic had started with Larry and spread to him or hit them both at the same time, he didn't know. Halfway along, the road went to the left and downhill, and here they ran even faster, Larry ahead now, looking scared, very scared, with the eyes and movements of a bolting horse.

Even although it was downhill, a point was quickly reached when they couldn't go any faster. Their hope was held back at the limits of their running: the limits of their hope were the limits of their bodies. Douglas strove to make it not so, but could not. Flat out. Perhaps then they should stop and recover themselves, out of their calamitous breathlessness decide what they should do?

As though his senses had been cleansed by panic, the violent running, Douglas was suddenly able to smell, acutely, smoke from the explosion, from chimneys and garden fires, grass and sap and foliage, petrol and oil, diesel, barbecues.

Larry now stopped, stumbling, hands on hips. They had about fifty yards to go to the end of the road. The road it joined was one of three which ran down to the town, the main square. They could hear shouts, then applause, then more shouts. Then silence, silence for the speeches, barely audible up here, mere broken threads of sound.

For a moment or two then, in the profound lull between energy violently spent and energy slowly returning, they might have been wondering why they had been running at all, never mind so fast, with such terrible abandon.

Then they saw Edith passing the end of the road in her wheelchair. She was alone and going downhill – quite fast. She was also, it seemed, on fire, ablaze. At first Douglas' thought was that because it couldn't really be so, it wasn't so. The flames were some kind of product of her velocity, harmless as dust.

He didn't think it for long because already she appeared to be recoiling from the flames, recoiling as in a dream, with incredibly stalled and slowed up movements.

What he thought next was that the very speed of her descent would put out the flames. Unless she ran into a wall or a car, she would be alright. As it was, the flames had been flattened by the wind of her passage, tucked about her like wild red feathers. If he ran fast enough, he might be able to put them out, one by one.

Shouting, screaming, running again. It was as if the run in the upper town had been a rehearsal. Douglas was sure he was keeping up with the wheelchair, gaining on it even. Soon he would have her in his arms again. He would take her home. She would tell them what had happened.

It was drawing away from them though, Edith was draw-ing away from them, heading for the main square, the crowds. Father and son redoubled their screams, frantic

to warn, to enlist help, inspire some miraculous interven-
tion. Twice the wheelchair veered and tilted, twice righted
itself. Or was righted by the burning Edith. They were run-
ning in its burning wake – too close and they might start
to burn also.

Larry was well ahead of him, Helen behind somewhere.
He didn't know how he could sprint like this.

The wheelchair ran along a level stretch of road for a
bit, but then, like a ski-jumper taking off, went over the
last hill before the square, leaving the ground as it did so.
He lost sight of it, but from changes in the noise of the
crowd – speeches faltering, shouts becoming screams, fer-
vour and good fellowship horror – he could tell that Edith
was approaching and would soon be at rest. The crowd
would surround her, he was sure, one or two great souls
stepping forwards to give aid.

He ran after Larry into the screaming crowd. The wheel-
chair had toppled over and was burning freely, high leap-
ing flames and dense black smoke. Edith had been thrown
from it and was sitting, in her own circle of fire, about
five yards away. Dark and getting darker, she was making
spidery little gestures as to a god of her own choosing. She
was swaying, a kind of charred vatic monkey. Then she
was even smaller, a midget woman being ushered from life
by extraordinary forces.

Larry was bellowing at her, his belief seeming to be that
her sacrifice was some malignancy of the will which only
pure rage could overcome. Douglas felt the same. For
some moments they bellowed together, until their voices
cracked and they were silent.

"It's almost over," Helen said behind them.

Moving forwards on his knees, Douglas put his arms
about his son, aware that the strange smell was that of
Edith burning.

"Almost over," Helen said again, her voice quiet and
still against the commotion, the sirens of the approaching

emergency services, already overwrought, overstretched on account of the earlier disturbance.

Edith's Journal – 7

Woken around three by terrible pain. Oddly I thought it was in the walls or the bedclothes at first rather than in me. No chance. Back with a vengeance. You'd have thought it could have waited another day, given me ... allowed me ...

Four now. Hard to write, but the pain drives me to. Who is whose instrument? Said it before: pain, mine anyway, seems to have a mind, purposes, a will. If some are chosen by God, some are chosen by pain. Don't ask me how you know the difference. Quite close, I suspect. Good to think so. Let me think so. Who will ever know?

In each joint and in lines between them the pain burns. Or are there several pains, vying with each other, competitors? I don't know. They seem to send each other messages. I can't decode these. Sometimes then I think – give me another perspective and I'd hear music. My body. Wracked, wracked into song! Terrifying harmonies. What would I understand, were I to hear them?

What a question: What nonsense: Let me hear them first!

So what must I do to hear them? Haven't I taken enough initiatives? Let them come to me! Yes!

Rage, irrationality – it gets you nowhere. There are no such songs. Screams more likely. Screaming children! I hear them behind me and before me and within me as I write.

Douglas is asleep. Not deeply or peacefully, of course. Who could possibly rest, given tomorrow? Larry's been up twice, once, as if tempted to come in, pausing by our door. I could hear his breathing. He must be feeling it all depends on him. It does, doesn't it? If we belonged to a primitive tribe, we'd be sleeping together, watched over by ancestors, no doubt.

Pain like this puts it out of the question. Watching from

the hilltop, I mean. I thought it'd be possible. Not now. Utterly. Waiting – except for the pain to cease – is impossible. You can't wait with pain. It mocks you.

Then it can make you feel you should be doing something with it. Not sure if this is mockery or good advice. It can make it seem as if its purposes are your purposes. If you but knew it, your purposes too (whatever they are)! God's? I see what you mean. If we've got this far, we might as well go the whole hog. (Who am I addressing?) I'll be glad to own up to them anyway, whatever they are, whether mine alone or ... another's also and in parallel somehow ...

In this matter of the march, the explosion. What has there been in it for me, if you stop to think about it? I'd have settled for it, I think, for a mother is blessed when she witnesses the fine purposes of her children bravely fulfilled. I would, oh almost surely so. But in spite of the pills and the brandy and the deep breathing and the thoughts of colourful and infinite horizons, it isn't enough and never now can be or will be. No. I can't rest. I cannot.

D'you know what I'm thinking? That the person suffering from great pain is like the person suffering from sexual desire. Quite similar sounds and movements, if you think about it. Abandonment the only answer. To orgasm for them, for me ...?

The curtain trembles in a light breeze. It's quite hot, but maybe I'm slightly feverish. Normally with pain like this I can't write at all. I'm writing quite steadily, though, as if the pain is driving me more than ... the reverse. Can I write myself out of pain or am I just going forwards into further pain? Or am I not in pain at all, just crazy enough, self-absorbed enough, to think that I am? Pain! Pain! Pain! Can I not stop going on about it! Can I not cease and forever on the subject! There are others. Let me choose one. Let me see.

For five minutes there I neither moved nor wrote. I had the illusion that I could hear all the insects in the garden, all the birds and animals on the moor, hushed nocturnal sounds, intimate adjustments. Once heard the base too, some stridency or other followed by a shout.

Douglas stirs, turns, but does not wake. May he sleep on. Tomorrow will tax us all. Should I wheel myself through to see Larry, talk to him if he's awake, sit by him until dawn if he isn't? I'd do it only it would wake Douglas.

Writing the above, an image was flickering on the edges of my mind. It is doing so still, as I write this. In the darkness of my pain or my unconscious. It's in fragments, struggling to come together. An image in the making. Presently it will come forwards, over a threshold of faith and pain, and I will see it, it will be revealed, or will reveal itself.

Perhaps not much though. Not much will be revealed, I mean. It's always possible. You sweat to give birth, or to make birth possible, and are disappointed. Nothing appears at all or it is banal. You'd have thought I'd have learnt by now not to expect much, not to court revelation even as I go on about the likelihood of nothing or of damn little. I'm doing what I'm doing though. I'm waiting. May not be making much sense but I'm waiting. Or am awaited. (Am awaited?)

Not quite sure what this is that I'm seeing. It could be a donkey, down on its front knees, performing a trick of some kind. The movements are slow, as though it's spellbound. There seems to be a crowd. Yes, it has an audience. Then I see a human head, attached to this body, a centaur it would seem, though I hope not, for what would be the point of that? The head is bald, that of an old man, wise-looking, shrunken. The legs are kicking however; the legs are disturbed. Between the upper and lower halves no accord at all. Then I see nothing. As well nothing as a centaur, if that's all it was. At a time like this to be bothered by centaurs. God preserve.

Then I see it. At last! A newsreel from the sixties. In protest against the Vietnam War a Buddhist monk is burning himself to death. In a pyre of his own making he is swaying backwards and forwards, backwards and forwards, his gestures at once of supplication and farewell. He is bald, with spectacles, rather like Gandhi, and he is not afraid. He is in slow motion, dying very patiently while policemen, soldiers, businessmen and other monks look on. Charred then, brittle, he falls to one side, is still. There are screams, I think, but not from him. He is beyond us now.

If pain has driven me to this vision, the vision has certainly subdued the pain.

So that's the idea for me today? Really? Bribe a passing youngster to go and buy some petrol, then set fire to myself on my hilltop?

Seems so.

Is there no other way?

X

They continued to smell her after her death and even after the funeral. Believed they did, anyway. It was not just a smell but a presence, suddenly there, as suddenly gone. It would come at them in the hall, the lavatory, in the middle of the night, at dawn. Douglas believed they must have it in their hair, their clothes, the car, on their very flesh. He would wring his hands, look over his shoulder.

Larry thought that if they were to scatter her ashes in some beautiful and appropriate spot, the smell would leave them, they would be free of it. He suggested the top of a mountain; he suggested the loch.

Though Edith had occasionally talked of mountains – dream talk, much of it, corries, ridges, summits as places of transcendence, redemption – they didn't think they had the strength or daring for them at the moment. Most of them still had snow and looked wintry even in the sunlight.

They chose the loch instead, a cove about a mile past Helen's cottage, meeting there early one morning to be sure of being alone.

Three times they tried to launch the urn on the waters of the loch, three times it was brought back to them, bobbing stubbornly. It got caught amongst rocks, amongst seaweed, amongst detritus. Vexed, Douglas seemed about to call the ceremony off, if ceremony it was.

"We can't give up," Larry said. "Nature isn't made to order. I may have to help it on its way – throw it, I mean, toss it."

"You can't throw an urn," Douglas objected. "It would be farcical."

"She wouldn't mind, I assure you. That way it would be sure to catch the right currents and be taken out to sea. Look, there, where the dark water is, that's the place, there are strong currents there, it's very deep."

He made as if to take the urn from his father, but Douglas backed away, holding it behind his back, mouthing distress, annoyance. Larry desisted, also backing away. In the early morning warmth of the cove it appeared that the venture had come to grief. Gulls cried and swooped and on the still air there was an immense smell of sea, the pungent salt wrack of it, the oiliness.

"It doesn't need to be irreverent," Helen said simply. "I'm sure Larry has a good arm."

And so it proved. As if silence had lent itself to them for a moment or two, they didn't hear Larry throw the urn, didn't hear it sail through the air, didn't hear it hit the water. They were simply aware of it after it had come to rest, bobbing a little before one of the strong currents Larry had spoken of bore it away.

By the start of the summer Douglas was alone in the cottage. As if the time had come for father and son to mourn separately, Larry had taken a temporary job with the forestry commission in Dumfriesshire.

Douglas had lived in the cottage for less than a year.

Mourning on his own, it turned out, was easier than mourning with Larry. He wasn't required to console, to concern himself with a grief which, he suspected, was deeper and more terrible than his own.

He gave way to the strangest impulses, though, pushing the spare wheelchair round the house, for example, as in search of Edith, bending low over it and saying things, what he hardly knew; pushing it out into the garden, weeping, calling her name, cursing the silence; once pushing it angrily away from him, down a grassy slope, laughing when it came to rest, unbearably empty, against a hedge.

He found her journal (clearly she had intended him to, for it was in her desk), a red hardbacked book in which there were only seven entries. From entry to entry the handwriting had deteriorated, he noticed, parts of the last one barely legible.

In spite of its awful privacy, he took it as a kind of gift. He read it again and again, sometimes inside the house, sometimes outside, in the May sunshine, often weeping at the generosity of her thoughts and feelings, calling out to her. Why hadn't she been able to share them with him when she lived? Or was this in part what she had been doing? Through the apparent privacy of her journal she had been reaching out to him?

He did these things although he thought it possible that he was still being watched.

They had been questioned, Larry and he, Larry mainly about the explosion, Douglas about Edith's death. For a whole morning the cottage and garden had been searched, but nothing had come to light. (Douglas had hidden Edith's journal and Larry his manuals and tools.) There was nothing to link Larry with the explosion, and Edith's death was accepted by the procurator fiscal as suicide on account of illness and unsound mind.

However, as if the authorities believed it was only a matter of time before evidence emerged, before father and son did something incriminating, police or military vehicles drove past the cottage daily. Sometimes they went quickly, as if on their way somewhere else, sometimes slowly, as if about to stop. Once a police car stopped under a tree: for a whole hour a pair of binoculars was trained on the cottage. Douglas and Larry could see them glinting in the sun.

They were surprised by the blatancy of it. What was their game? Were they trying to scare them into a confession? Any confession better than none?

The surveillance seemed to stop when Larry went to Dumfriesshire. Douglas continued to look for signs of it, but didn't find any. This didn't entirely persuade him it had ceased, however. If he had been sharp enough, he suspected, he would have spotted it. But grief had slowed him down; some of his awareness had been blunted. Scenes and figures from the past were visiting him, haunting him. The present could take care of itself. They might still be keeping an eye on him, the police, the military, here and there, now and then. He just couldn't see it.

He didn't think it mattered really. Hadn't he deeper adjustments to make? Nevertheless, whenever Larry rang, which was three or four times a week, he gave him strong reassurances, not thinking he would come home without them.

Larry had been nervous as well as miserable since his mother's death, morbid actually, going so far as to blame himself for it. Had he not been so obsessed with the raft, the explosion, it wouldn't have happened. She wouldn't have been driven to such an extreme. More than likely he had given her a taste for extremes. More than likely he had.

Douglas tried to calm him, himself as well, by saying that it was clear from the journal that it was the years of pain and illness that had given her a taste for extremes, extremes of martyrdom at that. What she had tried to do was sublimate her pain, use it in the service of mankind. A kind of horrific apotheosis. That was how they should see it. The terms of the journal should be the terms of their appreciation. And they were high terms.

He would read parts of the journal over the phone to Larry, aware as he did so that his son was sometimes weeping, sometimes sobbing. He read on because there was nothing else for it, because he was sure also that Edith would have wanted it. Her journal was her story, the last part of her life. She had left it to them.

He didn't seek Helen out much, but was pleased to see her whenever she called, which was every two or three days. Usually they went out somewhere, Helen driving. She talked about her cottage, her plans for it, what it was like to live there after the city. She talked about the sounds on waking, the smells, the light. She might have been trying to ease him, he thought, so simply did she speak.

Either this or she spoke about Edith. The manner of her death had humbled her. She acted as if, for the time being, it was the measure of all things, her own contribution on the day of the march, paltry, insignificant, vain. She was desperate to hear about her, almost anything at all. Douglas was glad to oblige, for above all he wanted to talk about this woman who had been his wife.

Doing so, however, he could become confused: was he talking to Helen in the presence of Edith, or to Edith in the presence of Helen? To the living and the dead, both, he seemed to be paying court.

One morning she took him along the coast to where a fishing boat, its net allegedly entangled with a submarine, had been sunk, its crew of three lost. The local community was demanding an inquiry, compensation, the Americans were denying liability. She had been to the scene three times already, she said. Two bodies had been washed ashore, and Douglas had the odd impression that Helen wanted to be the one to find the third. She spoke of how the shore there would receive bodies; of how they would rock gently backwards and forwards on tidal backwaters, waiting; of how bodies found in water on a quiet shore would be less shocking than bodies found in basements, streets, hillsides, undergrowth. It was as if she had made a study of it, was preparing to offer herself to the local community as some kind of helper, expert. A way of announcing herself, the new owner of the cottage beneath the cliff.

They parked the car above the cove where the bodies had been found. A small group of locals stood on the beach round a fire. They weren't talking, just standing about, a kind of vigil. Two of them nodded when Helen got out of the car. Douglas wondered if their protest was already running out of steam. Then one of them called out to Helen that in the local paper the Americans had been accused of war games, of playing with the fishing boats, using them in their manoeuvres. Helen answered that it didn't surprise her; it would have surprised her had it not been so. Hands in pockets, she moved towards the fire a little, stopped. A cold wind was blowing.

When she moved on, it was purposefully, taking Douglas to the spot between two rocks where, propped in a sitting position apparently, one of the bodies had been found. As if it was she who had discovered it, she made sinuous movements with her hands as she spoke.

"The last body may be found miles away," Douglas said. "Or not at all. It sometimes happens."

"I know. But it's important he should be found. He was married, with three young children."

He would have said that, when he opened his mouth to speak, it was to persuade Helen to come home. It was too cold to be out; a bank of dark clouds was moving in from the sea – soon there would be rain as well as wind. Also, he didn't want her to be disappointed: quite obviously she was hoping to be invited to stand by the fire and discuss the recent outrage, make plans.

When he spoke, however, it was to encourage her in her search for the body, to commend her, her patience and concern, her radicalism, low grade and borrowed though it might be. He heard himself suggest that they walk along the shore for a mile or two, searching. Surprised by his mood of willingness, wanting to act on it while it lasted, he turned his jacket collar up and, taking her by the hand, set off.

Since Edith's death, he had got used to this sort of thing, to being surprised by himself, his moods, initiatives. Of all the strange things he had done, though, this was probably the strangest. Their chances of finding the body were remote, but here he was, diligent amongst rocks and seaweed, pools and backwaters, giving it a try.

If he had embarked on the search as a kind of game, a way of humouring Helen, it wasn't long before he was taking it seriously. From diligence to gravity: he noted it in himself.

The wind was getting colder, it was becoming very overcast, and a group of fishing boats, in solidarity with the dead, was moving towards the base, flags flying.

Quite suddenly then Douglas had the sense that their presence on the shore, the locals in quiet vigil about the fire, the fishing boats in protest on the loch, were necessities, hard and radiant beyond mere contingency. It seemed to dignify him. He moved with a kind of strenuous gravity, looking left and right, stopping, going forwards a few yards, stopping again, checking behind rocks, in pools, going forwards once more.

The arrival of the rain, far from deterring him, made him quite as urgent in his searches as Helen. His strides were vigilant and disciplined, perfectly adapted to the conditions, and it was perhaps for this reason indeed that he had the intermittent illusion that he was pushing Edith in her wheelchair. Once he actually leant forwards slightly as though to try and catch what she was saying or to say something himself.

Helen had a pair of binoculars with which, every five minutes or so, she would scan the loch, the shoreline. When she spotted anything, she would raise her left hand and call to Douglas to come and check whether what she was seeing was a tyre, a crate, a buoy, a body.

When the fishing boats came back, rolling and pitching, still in formation, they looked at them too through the binoculars. The crew were in yellow mackintoshes, standing to attention beneath the vigorous flags as the boats, as though self-driven at this time of grief, moved steadily towards the bank of dark clouds.

It started to rain heavily. They left the shore and made for a wood, sheltering there for about half an hour while the rain fell angrily through the foliage into the earth about them. The loch was heaving, the line between water and sky indistinguishable now, and the fishing boats were moving in and out of mist and darkness.

"The fire won't survive this," Douglas said.

"No. But they'll be back on duty as soon as they can."

"There are always causes," Douglas offered, believing that Edith had said something like it in her journal. "We don't have to look far."

But Helen was glued to the binoculars again. Even from here and in the poor light Douglas could see that what attracted her attention was a seal, not a drowned fisherman.

He wasn't sleeping well. Either he couldn't get off at all or he would wake suddenly (once, convinced that Edith was in the room, calling for him) and be unable to sleep again. He took to visiting his observatory around midnight, staying there until three or four when he would go to bed and sleep for a few hours, waking, if not refreshed, then alert, sanguine before the day.

In the first two weeks of June there was a succession of clear nights after hot days. It was still warm as he made his way up to the observatory. Moths and fireflies greeted him at the door, bats were about, and there were rabbits, undone by the heat, barely moving.

Setting up the telescope, he felt the heat of the day in the wooden walls and roof, and, if he trained it on a cottage or a boat, he was aware of haze, shimmering, distortion. When he trained it on the sky, however, he was aware of no such interference. Distant space seemed clearer and steadier than his own locality, purer. He felt its coolness, from the troubled heat of his earthly frame felt it keenly.

He had been observing Andromeda for five nights, but tonight the Great Square of Pegasus at its western end was clearer than he had ever known it. One of the great constellations of early summer, two sides of the square were pointing towards the Pole Star. He didn't know why he was dwelling on it quite so ardently, with such expectation, and he didn't know why he had begun to speak the names of the stars out loud. Algenib and Markab, the names of the bottom stars of the Great Square, he uttered several times with grand emphasis.

Sailors dependent on them for navigation, he thought, might have spoken them thus. Algenib, Markab. Great presences. He tried to study them silently, but soon he was speaking the names again and in a voice not quite his own, he felt. Incantatory, as though someone was speaking through him, it seemed to issue from abnormal depths, his whole body quivering. Sweat gathered in his eyes; the end of the telescope grew moist. He had to step outside for a few moments, into the close darkness.

Around four he went down to the cottage, but instead of going to bed, he made himself a meal. He hadn't been eating well and this sudden hunger surprised him. He even laid a place for himself at the kitchen table. He ate meditatively, with gratitude, an omelette, a salad, fruit salad, remembering the time after his heart attack when he had rediscovered food.

He looked out into the garden as he ate, seeing that the short summer night was almost over. Released from the shades, Larry's hut was a presence again, seemed to be asking for attention, use.

When the phone rang then, he was as prepared for it, he thought, as he would ever be. If it was a friend, he would tell them about Andromeda and Pegasus; he would speak the names Algenib and Markab. Would be glad to. Midsummer equanimity. The sort of night which kept people up, made them take note of their world. Possible to think that even the careless would be moved to see that the stars were close, the earth warm.

If it was an enemy, he found himself thinking, it wouldn't make any difference: he would still talk about Andromeda and Pegasus. Why not? For the time being he had few other thoughts. Truly spoken, Algenib and Markab might carry the day.

He spoke into the receiver fearlessly, giving his number. There was no reply. He spoke his number again. Still no reply. He thought it might be Larry, drunk and desperate, struggling in a phone box or someone's home. He waited. Still no answer, but he could tell, from a certain fullness, openness, that the line was alive and that there was someone there.

A click then: the line was dead, leaving him with the feeling that he had been looked over and found, if not wanting, then irregular somehow, out of step.

Though it was almost light, he went up to the observatory again. He loved to watch stars disappear, dissolved as by light and distance. As a child, he had had the fancy that when dawn broke the stars sped to the outer reaches of the universe, there to be consumed and replaced, the following night, by other stars. To see the Great Square of Pegasus fade, the air softening about the hooded earth, was to be quietened. It was easy then to fold up the telescope, lock the hut and go down to bed. Sleep would follow.

He was surprised in his descent by the sight of a car. It was stationary, parked off the road a little past the cottage. He couldn't see if there was anyone in it. Nestled into the hillside, it looked as if it had been there all night. It wasn't a navy car or a police car, but that didn't mean anything. It was harder than ever these days to know what was what, who was who. There seemed no end to the forms of disguise and masquerade.

It worked both ways, of course. Whoever was in the car

might be thinking that Douglas' observatory was a cover for something else. In parts of the world like this, there was no reason to trust appearances. None at all.

He went deliberately down the hill through the luminous dawn, keeping his eye on the car. When he reached his garden, he set up the telescope between two trees and went down on one knee.

He could discern dim shapes in white shirts, a match flaring, movements, also something glinting, binoculars perhaps. In the lee of the hill, nothing was clear. Probably why it had been chosen, he thought. Tactics. The necessity of tactics.

The deadliness of mutual scrutiny. Stalemate. Too ridiculous to unnerve.

Laughing, he stood up, folded the telescope and went inside.

He was woken by the phone just after nine. It was Helen, asking him did he want to go for a picnic, it was such a beautiful day. He agreed, thinking that today almost any of her suggestions would have seemed inspired.

Still in pyjamas, he went outside. The air was balmy, the loch without ripples, like glinting tin, and the sky cloudless.

The car had gone, the place where it had stood bright and clear, a lay-by merely. Perhaps they had been a courting couple, overwrought by midsummer, unable to keep their hands off one another.

The phone rang again, Larry this time, wondering if it would be all right if he came home for a short visit in ten days' time. Apart from anything else, he had his court case. And there was a girl, Belinda, he wanted his father to meet.

"You'll like her."

"I'm sure I will."

"We won't be disturbing you, Helen and you, I mean?"

"Not at all. Delighted."

"Not moved in yet, has she?"

Douglas laughed.

"Moving in maybe but not moved in. That'll take time. Months."

"You're sure?"

"Dead sure."

"See you then."

"Sure. Take care."

He went outside again, for it was indeed a beautiful day, unusually quiet for that part of the world.